THE CAMBRIDGE BIBLE COMMENTARY

NEW ENGLISH BIBLE

GENERAL EDITORS

P. R. ACKROYD, A. R. C. LEANEY, J. W. PACKER

UNDERSTANDING
THE NEW TESTAMENT

UNDERSTANDING
THE NEW TESTAMENT

EDITED BY
O. JESSIE LACE

CAMBRIDGE UNIVERSITY PRESS

CAMBRIDGE

LONDON · NEW YORK · MELBOURNE

Published by the Syndics of the Cambridge University Press
The Pitt Building, Trumpington Street, Cambridge CB2 1RP
Bentley House, 200 Euston Road, London NW1 2DB
32 East 57th Street, New York, NY 10022, USA
296 Beaconsfield Parade, Middle Park, Melbourne 3206, Australia

Library of Congress catalogue card number: 65–19153

ISBN 0 521 04205 4 hard covers
ISBN 0 521 09281 7 paperback

First published 1965
Reprinted 1969 1973 1979

Printed in Great Britain at the
University Press, Cambridge

GENERAL EDITORS' PREFACE

The aim of this series is to provide commentaries and other books about the Bible, based on the text of the New English Bible, and in these various volumes to make available to the general reader the results of modern scholarship. Teachers and young people preparing for such examinations as the General Certificate of Education at Ordinary or Advanced Level in Britain and similar qualifications elsewhere, have been especially kept in mind. The commentators have been asked to assume no specialized theological knowledge, and no knowledge of Greek or Hebrew. Bare references to other literature and multiple references to other parts of the Bible have been avoided. Actual quotations have been given as often as possible.

This volume is designed to provide in somewhat greater detail the background information which is needed for the study of the books of the New Testament and which can only be sketched in very brief form in the separate commentary volumes. It outlines the larger historical background, says something about the growth and transmission of the text, and tries to answer the question 'Why should we study the New Testament?' It is linked also by its content with another volume, *New Testament Illustrations*, which provides in the form of maps, diagrams and photographs information which also supplements the commentaries. Both these volumes have been planned with the commentary series in mind, but are quite independent of it, and it is hoped that they will be useful to other readers as well.

P.R.A.
A.R.C.L.
J.W.P.

EDITOR'S PREFACE

Chapter 2 owes much of its material to the Reverend H. St J. Hart of Queens' College Cambridge, who has permitted the editor to make use of a first draft of a book he is preparing on the history and thought of the period between the Testaments. He has also given much time to answering queries and making suggestions for the improvement of the chapter, but the editor takes full responsibility for its final form.

The editor wishes also to express gratitude to the other contributors to the volume and also to the General Editors of the series for their help, as well as to her colleagues at William Temple College.

O.J.L.

CONTENTS

CONTENTS

3   HOW THE NEW TESTAMENT CAME INTO BEING

By *C. F. D. Moule*

viii

CONTENTS

4   HOW THE NEW TESTAMENT CAME TO US

By *J. N. Birdsall*

LIST OF ILLUSTRATIONS

1

WHY WE STUDY THE NEW TESTAMENT

THE BIBLE AND THE CHURCH

The book called the Bible is about sixteen hundred years old and parts of it are much older than that. But of course it has not been obtainable in English for anything like so long. Very few books either old or new get translated out of the languages in which they were originally written; when people set out to do this very difficult job it must be for an important purpose. The Bible has now been translated into more languages than any other book and this has been done with the idea that the people who use all these different languages shall be able to read it, or at any rate hear it read, in their own language.

We take all this very much for granted but perhaps it is worth stopping to ask why it has been done. Would it not have saved a lot of trouble if the few people who can read the book in the original languages just told the rest of us what is in it? Some people do believe that this would be the best thing and that specialists should be trained and made responsible for doing it. But many more have held the opposite view and a lot of hard work has been put into translating the Bible. This has been done so that people could know the Bible in their own language; though when you look at some of the English translations which are still used they do not give this impression because the English is so different from what we use today. English, like every living language, changes just because it is alive and that is why a new translation, the New English Bible,

I

is being made now and why in years to come others will have to be made for our descendants.

Before translations are made, ordinary people can see and listen to the Bible only in a language strange to them. This was how it was in Europe before the reawakening of interest in scholarship, which we call the Renaissance, in the sixteenth century. The Bible was used, of course, in church; but it was in a Latin translation and the service was in Latin and the congregation had to depend on the clergy if they wanted an explanation in their own language. It seems that the time came when even some of the clergy were not sufficiently well educated to give this, and so the Bible had practically become a closed book. Then two things happened, both of which helped to bring it to life again. In the fifteenth century, manuscripts (hand-written copies) of Bibles in the original languages of Hebrew and Greek were brought into Europe and this was a great incentive to scholars. At the same time there was an urgent demand from some groups of people in the Church that the Bible should be translated into the languages of their own time so that it could be understood by people who did not know any of the old languages.

There had been some translations into English before this but they had not come into general use because they belonged to the early attempts to reform the Church. These early attempts were very unpopular with the authorities and they had been ruthlessly suppressed. All the writings associated with them were destroyed, except for the ones that were hidden away and not found till afterwards.

READING THE BIBLE

Eventually, however, great changes were made, especially during the Reformation in the sixteenth century. The most obvious practical result of the reforms in England was that services were held in English and the Bible too was translated so that it could be open to everybody. It was not open in the sense that everybody could read it for himself because even at that time only a few people could read at all. But it was open in the sense that clergy and other educated people had an English translation which they could use and which other people could hear and enjoy. By this time printing had been invented and that meant that many more copies could be made available more easily. The translating had been done by scholars and it was agreed that they had made a good version of the original as they knew it. In 1611 the translation which is still known in England as the Authorized Version was published and in their preface the translators said:

When Your Highness [King James] had once out of deep judgment apprehended how convenient it was, that out of the Original Sacred Tongues, together with comparing of the labours, both in our own, and other foreign Languages, of many worthy men who went before us, there should be one more exact Translation of the holy Scriptures into the English Tongue; Your Majesty did never desist to urge and to excite those to whom it was commended, that the work might be hastened, and that the business might be expedited in so decent a manner, as a matter of such importance might justly require.

This translation is also known as the King James Version and it was a magnificent piece of work. It has commanded great respect and deep affection and the hopes of those who sponsored and produced it have certainly been

3

fulfilled over a long span of time. It has remained virtually unchallenged as the English Bible until relatively recent times. In the nineteenth century, when there began to be much more education, this Bible was used a good deal in schools as well as churches and got to be much more widely known than before. Quite a lot of it is fairly familiar, people have a general idea they know what is in it; sometimes they quote it, quite often they *mis*quote it.

But the wording, the structure of the sentences, everything about that preface sounds very strange now; we almost need to translate it. And in the translation itself many words and phrases are no longer used in English, or are used in different ways. For example, in Mark 10: 14 'Suffer the little children to come unto me' is now 'Let the children come to me'; in Acts 7: 20 Moses is described as 'exceeding fair' but now as 'a fine child'; in 1 Pet. 4: 5 'the quick and the dead' is now 'the living and the dead'. A language which is alive and being used is bound to change; the faster the rate of social change the more rapidly the language changes. Those seventeenth-century translators said it was 'convenient' that there should be 'a more exact Translation'. We would not say that now; we would say that 'a new translation is a good idea'. The last three hundred years have seen very great changes of every kind and for some time it has been urgent that there should be a new English translation.

THE NEW ENGLISH BIBLE

The urgent need for this is not only because the English of this century is so different from that of the seventeenth. Changes in language are not the only changes which have to be taken into account. By the end of the nineteenth century so many more early manuscripts had been found and so much new light had been shed on the old ones that some revision of the 1611 version was essential. Scholars both in England and America worked on this and the English Revised Version of the New Testament was published in 1881, of the Old Testament in 1885, and the American Standard Version was published in 1901. But these people were not making a new translation; two of the principles laid down for the guidance of the English revisers were:

1. To introduce as few alterations as possible into the Text of the Authorised Version consistently with faithfulness.

2. To limit, as far as possible, the expression of such alterations to the language of the Authorised and earlier English Versions.

So naturally the language still sounds just as old-fashioned. The American version of 1901 has been further revised and was published as the Revised Standard Version in 1952. But the New English Bible which is being produced now is a new translation; a translation into the language which is used now and using words in the meanings which they have now. This gives people a much better chance of understanding what they are reading, but there is more to it than just the words used. All the books in the Bible are old; they were written a long time ago and translating them into modern languages does not translate them into modern ideas or even by itself clarify the meaning of the old ideas.

PREPARING TO READ THE NEW TESTAMENT

While the new information about early manuscripts has been coming in we have been gathering information about a lot of other subjects which help us to understand the ideas. We have learnt a lot about the life and history of the first Christians, how their beliefs crystallized in the early days. Besides this we have discovered a good deal more about the general background of New Testament times which helps to show what sort of impression Christianity must have made then. It looks as though the writers did not always find it easy to explain themselves clearly and simply even to their contemporaries, but it is not hard to understand the reason for this. They were writing about something which had almost completely overwhelmed the first disciples, so it is not surprising that they were sometimes at a loss for words, even when they were writing about it later on. They were absolutely certain that the death of Jesus had not been just the tragic end of a powerful and attractive teacher who had become unpopular with the authorities. Nor did they think that he had been just another unsuccessful Messiah (Hebrew for an anointed leader; the Greek translation is Christ). They believed that God had raised Jesus from death and that he was alive amongst them and working with them. This was the only way they could find to interpret their experience.

It was not only people who had known Jesus in what is generally called his earthly life who believed these things. The Church grew because others who had not been amongst his followers were convinced by the apostles' proclamation. They joined the company and shared its new life. Their certainty that Jesus is alive was a strong bond of fellowship amongst them: they were thrilled and excited by it and they thanked God for it. But it involved more than that. Because they believed that God had raised Jesus from death they believed that something new was actually happening. They expected that a final great climax would come quite soon. No wonder they wanted to share all this with other people and no wonder they had some difficulty in expressing themselves.

We can understand better what they were saying when we know more about what people believed in those days and what they were hoping for: we can see how important the Christian proclamation was to people and why it was such tremendously good news. We realize too how difficult it must have been to see, after the first shock of excitement, just what difference it was going to make in practice. They compared what was being proclaimed with what they had expected and because the proclamation partly agreed with the expectation they thought it would continue to do so. Because they had expected the coming of the Messiah to be just before the end of the world and they believed that Jesus was the true Messiah they thought the end of the world would be very soon. But the end of the world did not come. When they found that life was going on longer than they had expected, they began to think more about what practical differences their new beliefs were going to make. This is what has been going on ever since. Christians look at the world in which they live in the light of their belief that God maintains it and ceaselessly cares for it and desires the well-being of all its inhabitants. The Jews had already learned to believe this and they believed too that God had made an agreement, or covenant, with their ancestors. This was associated for them with their obligation to keep the

Jewish Law; the trouble was that they knew they had failed to keep it.

Christians say that God has made a new covenant. The word 'testament' is another word for covenant, or agreement. The New Testament means the new covenant, or agreement, which God made through Jesus Christ. The phrase came to be used as a title for the collection of books which tell us about how it was made and what it means. Over and over again Christians have to think out how this applies to their own times and discover how to proclaim this message of good news so that it can be recognized for the good news it is. The message is handed down in the traditional language and it is proclaimed sometimes in the old phrases, sometimes in new interpretations. Language changes, conditions change; but the proclamation is always a proclamation about God and what he has done.

'Are you the only person staying in Jerusalem not to know what has happened there in the last few days?' 'What do you mean?' he said. 'All this about Jesus of Nazareth,' they replied, 'a prophet powerful in speech and action before God and the whole people; how our chief priests and rulers handed him over to be sentenced to death, and crucified him. But we had been hoping that he was the man to liberate Israel. What is more, this is the third day since it happened, and now some women of our company have astounded us: they went early to the tomb, but failed to find his body, and returned with a story that they had seen a vision of angels who told them he was alive' (Luke 24: 18–23).

The New Testament has been so important in the life of the Church for all these centuries because in it there is the witness of the first people who believed and proclaimed these things. The books have been studied and

cherished and translated because people have believed
that what is proclaimed there about God and his dealings
with men is true. The Church has always harked back to
the authority of the New Testament both because the
evidence is there and because as time has gone on more
and more people have become more and more convinced
of the truth of it. It is because the New Testament is this
kind of book and not just a great moral classic or hero
story that it has to be studied in this special way. To help
to do this we have the New English Bible and the
Cambridge Bible Commentary, with this book of general
introduction telling about the historical, cultural and
religious background, about how the books came to be
written and about how they have been transmitted to us.

Most people who come to the study of the New
Testament already have some ideas about Jesus Christ.
The purpose of real study is not just to find support for
the ideas which we already have but to examine them,
probably to add to them and to investigate the basis of
them all and try to discover why they have been such a
powerful influence in history for all these centuries. The
social and cultural background of the twentieth century
is in most parts of the world very different from that of
the countries on the shores of the Mediterranean two
thousand years ago, but many of the questions men ask
are the same and many of the decisions they have to take
are about the same issues. Social and political problems
arise in new forms and religious questions are asked in
new words. The writers of the New Testament books
believed that what they were writing about was of fundamental, timeless significance for man's understanding of
himself and of his history. The books were not written
before a lot of discussion had gone on about the meaning

of 'all this about Jesus of Nazareth' and it has gone on ever since amongst scholars and amongst ordinary people as well. It is going on still, and over and over again the New Testament itself is re-read and thought about in relation to new questions as they arise. It is exciting to be doing this in the second half of the twentieth century when so much new help is available to many more people.

2

THE HISTORICAL BACKGROUND OF NEW TESTAMENT TIMES

In the year 400 B.C. the Persians ruled over a large empire. They had overrun the Babylonian empire but in the north-west they still held a frontier with the Greeks, although the Greeks had defeated them in Greece nearly a century earlier at the battles of Thermopylae and Marathon. When the Persians took over territories from peoples they conquered, including the Babylonians, they found themselves ruling over a very mixed population. Many of the people living in those territories had been transported, or their parents or grandparents had been, from their home country to another land.

On three occasions early in the sixth century B.C. people from Jerusalem and Judah had been taken to Babylonia (Jer. 52). Some had been deported, some taken as prisoners, some went as refugees. This kind of thing happened to the Jews and to many other peoples, but only the Jews kept in exile a sense of national and religious identity. The Jews kept alive their ancient traditions, whether eventually they returned home or remained scattered abroad as part of what came to be known as the 'dispersion'. They maintained strong loyalties, loyalty to one another, loyalty to the home country and Jerusalem in particular, loyalty to their religion. This religion was built on a strong belief in the mutual obligations of loyalty between the God whom their forefathers had worshipped as Yahweh and his people Israel.

Groups who had preserved their identity were encouraged by the Persians to go back and resettle in the lands of their forefathers and to establish a national life, including the practice of the national religion. This nationhood did not include political independence, and Persian officials were in authority throughout the Persian domain. By 400 B.C. this policy had been in operation for some time, and a small number of Jewish enthusiasts had taken advantage of it and were building up a new social and religious life in Jerusalem based on their own Jewish ideas and beliefs.

Since King Zedekiah had been taken captive to Babylon in 586 B.C. a lot of work had been done on the old Jewish traditions; many of them had been collected together and quite a number of the collections had been written down by 400 B.C. Minority groups develop strong loyalties, particularly if they are ruled over by a foreign power. For many Jews this loyalty was focused on the old traditions and on the books in which they were preserved, and so these books had come to be regarded as authoritative and holy. Holy, that is, in the sense of being a gift of God to his own People, as the Jews believed themselves to be, and in the sense of demanding utter obedience.

During Persian times a number of expeditions came from Babylon to Jerusalem, and about 400 B.C. a party came which included Ezra, a learned scribe. He set about teaching the people of Jerusalem their own Law which had been collected together and formulated by the exiles into something much more elaborate than what had survived after most of the leading people had been taken away from Jerusalem and Judah to Babylonia nearly two hundred years before. Not long before Ezra's time Nehemiah had got permission to leave the Persian court to organize the rebuilding of Jerusalem and its walls, and the life of the people living within them. These included some whose ancestors had never left, some who had come with earlier expeditions and some new arrivals.

Nehemiah and Ezra were able to reorganize the life and worship of the Jerusalem people according to the Law of Moses as some had come to interpret it. Their reforms were the triumph of a minority taking advantage of Persian policy and so committed to loyalty to Persian rule. Nehemiah had some controversy with the governor of Samaria, Sanballat, and refused any co-operation with the Samaritan people. Great emphasis came to be laid upon the Temple in Jerusalem and it was claimed that the Law laid down that sacrifices might be offered only there. The Samaritans could not agree to this but they continued to regard themselves as true Israelites although the Jews would not recognize them as such.

There were Jews living in other parts of the world as well, who had kept together and not inter-married with other peoples. There were many Jews in Palestine who were descended from those whom the Babylonians had left behind. There were Jews in Egypt, some who had gone there voluntarily, some as fugitives, some as soldiers. All the groups who had kept together had preserved and practised their own religion. When times were more peaceful or when the lands they lived in came to be ruled by one powerful empire, links were forged between these communities and they all shared to some degree in the fruits of the great work of gathering up and commenting on the Law which had been done in Babylon and elsewhere.

These Jews had a great common heritage but they were different in many ways from one another and frequently in the centuries immediately before Christian times the differences between them led to sharp controversy, sometimes even to armed conflict. Apart from extreme cases when other factors confused the main issues, it is generally true to say that these differences were so deep and so catastrophic because the underlying common conviction was so strong. All were agreed that God, the God whom their ancestors had worshipped, is one and supreme and that the rulership of the world is really his. But as things now are, the rule of God waits to be established. They were deeply divided about how it would come to be. Some thought they should wait, that no action was called for from them. Some thought they were called upon to act but were divided about time and place and method.

As, one after another, world empires overran Palestine the people learned to hope for freedom and prosperity in the future, always at some future moment when the ruling power was threatened from elsewhere and there might be a promising opportunity. Such hopes were never fulfilled, but they did not die; a succession of them can be traced from the fortieth chapter of Isaiah to the first chapter of Acts. There are many too in other Jewish books which are not in the Bible.

Not all Jews kept themselves separate nor were all loyal to their ancestral religion; those who were loyal to it became the only international people ever known and remain so to the present day. Wherever groups of Jews were to be found, whether in Palestine or in other countries, they practised circumcision as a custom marking their loyalty to God and to one another. They observed the sabbath, the seventh day of the week, as a day on which work was forbidden by the Law: the rules for the sabbath became very elaborate, as we can see in the New Testament. On the sabbath there was a meeting in the synagogue (a Greek word meaning a coming of people together) for the purpose of reading and exposition of scripture.

The custom of gathering together for prayer, praise, reading and exposition of scripture may have begun even before the Babylonian exile. Whenever it actually began the practice of meeting in the synagogue evidently became common during the Babylonian exile and subsequently throughout the Jewish dispersion. In the Law the Jews learned about their ancestors and the great things that God had done for them. They learned about Abraham and how God had promised great things to his descendants and that his descendants should be a blessing to the world (Gen. 12: 2, 3).

When the Law was expounded in the synagogue the people heard the regulations about the three great annual festivals in Jerusalem when the appropriate sacrifices were to be offered in the Temple. These were (a) the festival of Passover with which is associated the eating of unleavened bread, when firstfruits were offered and the Exodus commemorated; (b) the festival of Weeks, known as Pentecost, when firstfruits of wheat were offered; and (c) the festival of Tabernacles, at the time of the grape and olive harvest. Jews living away from Jerusalem came for these feasts if they could: many of them probably never could but large numbers did come, some travelling long distances in order to do so. There were other annual occasions besides the three great festivals, the sabbath was observed weekly, and every day offerings of incense were made, in the morning and evening. The priests took turns in carrying out this responsibility.

THE JEWS UNDER HELLENISTIC RULE

Alexander, a pupil of Aristotle the great Greek philosopher, succeeded his father Philip II as king of Macedon in 336 B.C. The independent city states of Greece, Athens, Sparta and others were too independent to survive against the organized military power of Macedon. The Macedonians brought to an end the inter-city wars of the Greek states before involving their soldiers in the eastern campaign. Alexander's conquest of the Persian empire, in the fantastically short period of eleven years, brought Macedonian-Greek rule to the East. Alexander hoped that his rule would be for the benefit of all who lived in the vast territories over which he so quickly came to rule. The Greeks had despised all those who did not speak Greek, 'barbarians' as they called them. Alexander shared the pride in all things Greek, which was well founded; but this led him not to despise others but to a desire that all should share these good things, the riches of the language and the opportunities of city life. Many of the conquered peoples were ready to welcome all of this and the great imperial territory began to get hellenized. This new culture, adopted largely from Greek thought and ways by people not themselves Greek, or Hellenic, is commonly described as hellenistic and those who actively sought it are called Hellenists.

Alexander crossed into Asia in 334 B.C. He died in Babylon in 323 B.C. having, at the age of thirty-two, become ruler of Egypt and of the Medes and Persians as well as king of Macedon. Plutarch, the Greek philosopher and biographer who lived about A.D. 50–120, reports that it was said of Alexander that 'he believed that he had a mission from God to harmonize men generally

16

GREEKS		JEWS	ROMANS
336 B.C. Alexander, King of Macedon 334 B.C. Alexander in Asia 323 B.C. Death of Alexander the Great			
SELEUCIDS	**PTOLEMIES**		
312/11-280 B.C. *Seleucus I*	323-285 B.C. *Ptolemy I*		
	285-246 B.C. *Ptolemy II*		
280-261 B.C. *Antiochus I*			
261-246 B.C. *Antiochus II*			
246-226 B.C. *Seleucus II*	246-221 B.C. *Ptolemy III*		
226-223 B.C. *Seleucus III* 223-187 B.C. *Antiochus III The Great*	221-203 B.C. *Ptolemy IV*		
	203-181 B.C. *Ptolemy V*		
198 B.C. Antiochus III victorious over Ptolemy V			
187-175 B.C. *Seleucus IV*			
189 B.C. Roman army victorious over Antiochus III at Magnesia-ad-Sipylum		168 B.C. Maccabaean revolt	
175-163 B.C. *Antiochus IV Epiphanes* 163-162 B.C. *Antiochus V* 162-150 B.C. *Demetrius I*	181-146 B.C. *Ptolemy VI*	165 B.C. Victory of Judas Maccabaeus Rededication of Temple 160 B.C. Death of Judas Maccabaeus at battle of Elasa 152 B.C. Jonathan Maccabaeus takes office as High Priest at the feast of Tabernacles 143 B.C. Jonathan captured at Ptolemais and put to death 134-104 B.C. John Hyrcanus 103-76 B.C. Alexander Jannaeus 75-66 B.C. Alexandra 67 B.C. Herod and Aretas march on Jerusalem	63 B.C. Pompey in Jerusalem 48 B.C. Battle of Pharsalus 44 B.C. Death of Julius Caesar 42 B.C. Battle of Philippi 40 B.C. The Romans turned out of Palestine by the Parthians
		37 B.C. Herod wins Palestine back from the Parthians. He reigns as king before the end of Herod's reign Birth of John the Baptist Birth of Jesus 4 B.C. Death of Herod the Great	31 B.C. Battle of Actium 27 B.C. Octavian becomes Augustus. He rules till A.D. 14 20 B.C. Parthians return the standards and the prisoners which they took in 40 B.C.

Fig. 1. A time chart of inter-Testament times.

17

and to be the reconciler of the world, bringing men from everywhere into a unity, and mixing their lives and customs, their marriages and social ways, as in a loving cup'.

Alexander had appointed no successor. In four areas of what had been the one empire, four generals took charge and competed for further power. Four separate hellenistic monarchies were thus established and strove against each other, a quick and sad decline from Alexander's vision of unity for mankind. The four kingdoms were Macedon, Thrace, Syria and Egypt. Although politically they were separate and in conflict, the whole of the eastern Mediterranean area was profoundly influenced by hellenistic culture and Greek became the common language. For the background of the New Testament we can confine our attention to two of these kingdoms: Syria, commonly called Seleucid Syria from the name of its first ruler, Seleucus; and Egypt, commonly called Ptolemaic Egypt from the name of its first ruler, Ptolemy. The majority of the succeeding kings of Egypt also had the name Ptolemy: the succeeding kings of Syria were mostly called either Seleucus or Antiochus. Many cities founded or rebuilt during the hellenistic period in Syria reflect these names, one called Seleucia and more than one called Antioch appear in the New Testament.

In the struggles after Alexander's death, Palestine came under the control of Ptolemy in Egypt and this was so until 198 B.C. A great city which Alexander himself had founded in Egypt, Alexandria, became one of the greatest centres of Greek learning and culture. As might have been expected, Alexander had settled people of different origins in this great city as a means of furthering the unity of mankind to which he was devoted. There was a con-

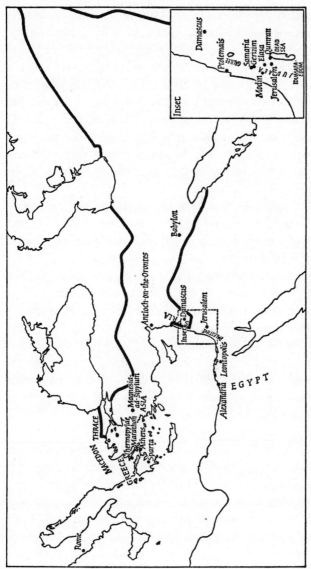

Fig. 2. The hellenistic kingdoms about 275 B.C.

Inset

Damascus
Ptolemais
GALILEE
Samaria
Gerizim
Elasa
Modin
Jerusalem
Qumran
DEAD SEA
IDUMAEA
EDOM

Babylon

Antioch-on-the-Orontes

CILICIA
Damascus
PALESTINE
Jerusalem
Inset

Alexandria
Leontopolis

EGYPT

MACEDON
THRACE
Thermopylae
Magnesia ad-Sipylum
Marathon
ASIA
GREECE
Athens
Sparta

Rome

siderable Jewish section in Alexandria; this community increased and became a centre of Jewish learning and culture. The Jews had strong beliefs, particularly strong beliefs about themselves, as a separate and chosen people, which were bound to clash with a general hellenizing policy which aimed at breaking down barriers of race and religion. But all the same there was fruitful interchange in cities like Alexandria as well as some fierce and bitter resistance. There was a cleavage amongst the Jews themselves, some willing to be very pro-hellenistic, some in very violent opposition.

Originally Judaism was a religion into which one must be born, but the time came when others could come into this fellowship by a process like naturalization. A non-Jew who became a Jew by religion, accepting its full obligations, was known as a proselyte (convert). These proselytes adopted all the practices of Judaism and they are included in the enumeration of the 'devout Jews drawn from every nation under heaven' (Acts 2: 5), 'Parthians, Medes, Elamites; inhabitants of Mesopotamia, of Judaea and Cappadocia, of Pontus and Asia, of Phrygia and Pamphylia, of Egypt and the districts of Libya around Cyrene; visitors from Rome, both Jews and proselytes, Cretans and Arabs' (Acts 2: 9–11).

Some non-Jews were attracted to the Jewish religion and adopted it. Many more respected the Jews for their loyalty to their faith and for the high standards of their behaviour. In many places the Jews earned special privileges. But they also inspired fear and dislike on account of their exclusiveness and superiority, and anti-Jewish feeling broke out in riots from time to time in Alexandria and elsewhere.

Exclusiveness was also evident in the affairs of Palestine.

It was probably during Alexander's time that the Samaritans built a Temple of their own on Mount Gerizim because the Jews would give them no share in Jerusalem.

THE SELEUCID KINGDOM

Seleucus I, the general who had taken control of Syria when Alexander died, had entered the city of Babylon in the year which we now call 312 B.C. From this year the years of this kingdom were counted and it marks the beginning of the Seleucid era. The writer of the first book of Maccabees is using this count when he refers to 'the hundred and thirty and seventh year of the kingdom of the Greeks' (1 Macc. 1: 10). In 300 B.C. Seleucus founded the city of Antioch on the Orontes, naming it in honour of his son, Antiochus, who succeeded him as Antiochus I. 'It was in [this] Antioch that the disciples first got the name of Christians' (Acts 11: 26).

In 198 B.C. Antiochus III, king of Syria, who came to be known as the Great, defeated the king of Egypt, Ptolemy V, so Palestine changed hands and Jerusalem came under Seleucid rule. Jerusalem was therefore affected by the fluctuations in the fortunes and the policies of the Seleucid family until the Romans drove out the Seleucids in 63 B.C. After Antiochus the Great had achieved his successes in the east and in the south he clashed with the Romans in the west and they defeated him in 189 B.C. at Magnesia-ad-Sipylum. The treaty which followed imposed an indemnity payment and demanded hostages. Charges of this kind always ultimately fall upon the peoples of the countries involved: when the people are subject people the taxes by which the necessary sums are collected are particularly unpopular. One of the hostages who was taken to Rome at this time was a young Antiochus who later ruled as Antiochus IV and who roused violent Jewish opposition.

JEWISH AFFAIRS, 321–168 B.C.

One important practical result of Alexander's conquests had been the spread of the Greek language. This does not mean that all the peoples stopped speaking their various national or local languages, but that they learned to speak Greek as well. Other languages had been used internationally before, for international affairs and in trading. Aramaic, the language of Aramaeans, or Syrians, was known by Persians and by Jews, but Greek became still more widespread and more generally used. In the cities it would be likely that Greek would be more commonly spoken: different peoples living more closely together would need a common language and Greek supplied it. In country districts the older, more familiar languages would be more regularly used. For ordinary purposes the Jews had used Aramaic for some time, although in worship Hebrew, the old language, was retained. But they learned to talk Greek, and by the middle of the third century B.C. it became necessary in Alexandria to have a translation into Greek of the Law (the five Books of Moses which come at the beginning of the Old Testament) for use in the synagogue. As time went on other books were translated as well. The Greek version of the Old Testament is commonly called the Septuagint, from the Latin word for seventy; the name comes from an old legend, told in the 'Letter of Aristeas' (see p. 36), about the translating. The word is generally abbreviated to the Roman numerals LXX.

Although the Jewish scholars who did the work were clear in their own minds about the meaning of the Hebrew they were rendering, and were very familiar with Greek, they found themselves in grave difficulty in the search for satisfactory equivalents. Everybody who has tried to translate from one language to another is aware of the problems of conveying exact meanings. In this case there were particular difficulties because words, including theological words, had different associations in the two languages. Thus, sometimes, in translating they felt it necessary to avoid words or ideas which might be mis-understood in a non-Jewish area. When, for example, they found God referred to as 'my rock' (Ps. 19: 14) they paraphrased it as 'my strength', perhaps for fear that any non-Jew might think that God was to be represented by a stone image. About a century before Christian times a Jew who was setting out to translate a book originally written in Hebrew wrote 'things originally spoken in Hebrew have not the same force in them, when they are translated into another tongue: and not only these, but the law itself, and the prophecies, and the rest of the books, have no small difference, when they are spoken in their original language' (Prologue to Ecclesiasticus).

A common language was spreading, a much more uniform way of life was growing up, but what about religion? It was discovered that a number of religions recognized one God only or at any rate put one god in a supreme position over others. Naturally people used, or had used, different names for this god in their different languages. Here was a real problem. It could be argued that these names were just different names for one and the same god: this would not matter so long as the things believed about him were the same. But if they were not the same there was a theological issue involved. Clashes of this kind appear most obviously in relation to the commands of gods. If one group of people believes that the supreme god demands human sacrifice and another group believes that the supreme god forbids this practice, it is obvious that the difference between them is much more than a difference of name.

Jews believed in one God, creator of the universe, who demanded righteousness from men; in different parts of the world they found themselves very differently placed in relation to the beliefs of their neighbours. In Alexandria, as we have seen, the scriptures were translated into Greek and there was a great deal of very fruitful conversation between scholars of different traditions and different religions. But Jerusalem was no new city and the Jewish population in it was far from homogeneous. It was a place to which Jews had come in Persian times with encouragement to rebuild the Jewish Temple and re-establish the Jewish religion. Those who responded to this encouragement had set about teaching the Jewish Law and fostering its observance. They still held to the view which had been emphasized in the time of exile, that Jews must keep themselves to themselves and must not marry others than Jews if they were to keep themselves as the pure People of God. Greeks regarded those who did not speak Greek as barbarians. Jews regarded those who did not worship God as unacceptable to God. The spread of the Greek language among barbarians was a vastly more straight-forward and rapid process than the breaking down of the barriers between Jews and non-Jews.

Far from being concerned for the unity which for Alexander had been a grand objective, the Jews who inherited the thinking of Ezra opposed any measures by which their traditions might be modified or their religion assimilated to any other. So in Judaism and particularly in Jerusalem there was an anti-hellenistic party. The conviction of being in a special way the People of God carried with it ideas about nationhood which made the anti-hellenistic party appear as the patriotic party. This attracted to it some elements whose primary concern was political independence over and above religious freedom.

Amongst the Jews themselves, in fact, a number of groups were beginning to form, marked off by the things they regarded as priorities, the issues which seemed crucial for each group. Those who stood in the Ezra tradition stood for strict observance of the Law and strict segregation from all who did not observe it as they believed it should be observed. They were a separatist group and their name, 'Pharisee', may actually mean 'separated'. They were separated not only from non-Jews but from those of their fellow-Jews who did not agree with them on all points. Now that the Jews were not politically independent and had no king of their own, the importance of the leading priests increased. They had taken over the religious functions of the king and developed the office of High Priest: the High Priest had thus become a key figure. Priests all came from the priestly families, of which there were a number, but there was no general agreement about which of these families were qualified for the office of High Priest. Some emphasized the importance of descent from Aaron; others insisted that the authoritative family was the descendants of Zadok, king David's priest in Jerusalem: these were called Sadducees, though the name may possibly have some other explanation.

SELEUCID TREATMENT OF THE JEWS

When Jerusalem came under the rule of Antiochus III in 198 B.C., he issued a decree which made clear his intention to encourage the Jews in the practice of their religion by protecting the Temple from non-Jews and by securing the supply of materials for the sacrifices in Jerusalem and also for the restoration of the Temple. He gave permission for the Jews to be governed by their own laws and excluded non-Jews from the holy Temple area. So it is not surprising that some Jews' response to this went beyond gratitude into positive enthusiasm. Antiochus found the Jews to be good and trustworthy soldiers and settled numbers of them with their families in places where there had been rebellion in Asia Minor. This was one of the ways in which it came about that Jews were already to be found in so many countries in the centuries immediately preceding New Testament times.

Antiochus III was succeeded by Seleucus IV who died in 175 B.C. It was he who had to pay the indemnity to Rome after the battle at Magnesia-ad-Sipylum, but he had also continued to pay the cost of the Temple sacrifices as his father had done. The High Priest in the reign of Seleucus was Onias III: but a certain Simon plotted against him hoping to get him removed from office. Simon suggested to the Seleucid government that there was money in the Temple, other than that set aside for Temple use, which might be made available. Heliodorus was sent to investigate and said that the money would be confiscated. This was prevented, but the threat horrified the people of Jerusalem.

When Seleucus IV died Onias withdrew to Antioch for safety and the new king, Antiochus IV, did not reinstate him as High Priest. Nor did he appoint Simon to the office. Onias's brother Jason (notice his Greek name) bribed the king to give him the appointment. Jason had the king's authority to introduce a new policy in Jerusalem—to remake it into a Greek city, to establish Greek education for the young men, including physical education in the gymnasium, possibly even to rename the city 'Antioch'. In this for the time being he had a certain amount of support. These institutions did not actually displace the Temple but they were a strong counter-attraction. Simon who had begun the moves against Onias had a brother, Menelaus, like him in character. He, though supposed to be working for Jason, offered the king a higher bribe and became High Priest. Jason fled, but only to await an opportunity to reinstate himself.

Before Antiochus IV, the Seleucid kings had not flaunted the customary Greek ideas about awarding divine honours to kings. But this Antiochus struck coins in his reign carrying the phrase 'Theos Epiphanes', 'God Manifest'. He is frequently known by this name of Epiphanes, in spite of the fact that its implication is violently denied by Jews, and equally of course by Christians.

Antiochus was determined on establishing himself as king in Egypt; he was temporarily successful. But when there came a rumour of his death Jason came to Jerusalem to reinstate himself by force and besieged the citadel where Menelaus was. Antiochus was not dead, however, and came to Jerusalem to quell this rebellion. Jason fled once more.

Before this time Antiochus had not actually interfered with the Temple itself, nor tried to break the power of the Jewish Law. But now he determined to destroy Judaism by attacking both of them. Claiming that the God of the Jews was the same as the Greek Zeus Olympios he ordered heathen altars to be erected in the Jewish cities and in the Temple at Jerusalem. The Law was prohibited. The penalty for resistance to these measures was death, but Jews were found who were willing to pay that price.

THE MACCABAEAN REVOLT, 168 B.C.

In the country in a village called Modin, not very far from Jerusalem, a priest called Mattathias, faithful to the Jewish religion, and who had refused to conform to the new regulations, killed a fellow-Jew who was in the act of sacrificing at the heathen altar which had been set up. Mattathias killed the sacrificer and the officer in charge, and tore down the altar itself.

This dramatic and dangerous protest encouraged many like-minded Jews to join Mattathias and his family in their flight to the mountains. But it was not possible to escape from Antiochus's agents and the refugees suffered bitterly. When Mattathias died, his five sons carried on the resistance to the king and the defence of their religion.

Judas was the first hero and leader of the organized and ultimately successful revolt. His prowess earned him the name of Maccabaeus, or Maccabee, which probably means Hammer, and the name remained with his brothers and with the whole movement. This is why the revolt is called the Maccabaean revolt. Yet the High Priest Menelaus and his associates were leading Jews, Jews whose willingness to accept hellenistic ways went far enough for them to be willing to obey the commands about sacrificing in heathen ways at heathen altars. So this war was in part a Jewish civil war in that on both sides the participants were Jews. Once hostilities had broken out, the family of Mattathias gathered the support of a number of parties in Judaism.

The family name of Mattathias was Hashmon and the family is therefore known as the Hasmonaeans; this family is important in Jewish leadership for several generations from this time.

The main group who came to the support of Judas Maccabaeus were called the Hasidaeans, or Chasidim. This name also was a nickname, meaning 'pious' or 'godly', and it was earned by their long-standing reputation for faithfulness to God and his Law. Since the beginning of the hellenistic era different groups of Jews had reacted differently to hellenizing policy. The differences were not altogether differences of degree but rather differences of opinion about the working out of the demands of loyalty. A moment of crisis for many was the time when the High Priesthood at Jerusalem fell into the hands of men who obviously had little concern for Judaism as such. The main body of Jews realized that leadership had fallen into the hands of men whom they were not able to respect, yet for a time they conformed and obeyed them.

When it became obvious that Judas and his party, now an army, were a real danger to the kingdom, he was attacked by an army under Lysias, acting for Antiochus who was away fighting in the east. But Judas was victorious and by 165 B.C. had occupied Jerusalem and the Temple itself. The Temple was restored and rededicated, the traditional priesthood re-established and the sacrifices reinaugurated. A feast of rededication was held and this became an occasion of annual remembrance, called Hanukkah (Rededication). 'The festival of the Dedication was being held in Jerusalem' (John 10: 22). Steps were also taken to restore the fortifications of Jerusalem so that city and Temple might be secure against any future threats.

The book of Daniel is generally supposed to have been written during these troubles, in fact at the height of them in about 167 B.C. The passage beginning at 11: 31 is a disguised account of Antiochus profaning the sanctuary. The purpose of the book is encouragement and two weapons are used, one is reference back to the past, the other visionary expectation of the future.

I saw in the night visions, and, behold, there came with the clouds of heaven one like unto a son of man, and he came even to the ancient of days, and they brought him near before him. And there was given him dominion, and glory, and a kingdom, that all the peoples, nations, and languages should serve him: his dominion is an everlasting dominion, which shall not pass away, and his kingdom that which shall not be destroyed (7: 13, 14).

In other words, the encouragement is the hope of super-natural intervention.

King Antiochus never returned to Jerusalem. He died in the east in 163 B.C. Antiochus V succeeded as king but Lysias ruled on his behalf and Antiochus remained in nominal power for only one year. Judaea was only one of many places where the Seleucid house was in trouble and a relatively minor one from their point of view; so all Judas's demands about religion were conceded. Menelaus who had bought the High Priesthood for a high price was executed and a new High Priest was appointed. This was Alcimus, a member of the family of Aaron, and evidently acceptable to the Hasidaeans (1 Macc. 7: 14). Nevertheless his sympathies seem to have been with the hellenizers. This appointment was only a compromise and neither side trusted Alcimus very far, so in spite of the re-establishment of the Temple and the Law the war was not over. When Lysias appointed Alcimus as High Priest there was another possible candidate, Onias IV, son of the Onias III who had been ousted by Simon in the reign of Seleucus IV. This younger Onias subsequently fled to Egypt with a number of Jewish soldiers and served there under the Ptolemies. They settled at Leontopolis and there Onias built a temple, a smaller copy of the one at Jerusalem, and established a sacrificial system. It survived for about two hundred years and shows that not all Jews believed that sacrifice could be offered only in Jerusalem.

At least from the point of view of Judas and his followers the war was not over, and their success and the obvious decline of Seleucid power encouraged them to fight on for complete independence. Many of the Jews ceased to support them, being satisfied with the freedom of worship which they had won and not wanting to be politically independent. There were also those Jews who believed that the People of God were called to political independence, indeed to world rule, but not by these means and methods.

RESISTANCE BY WITHDRAWAL

For some twenty years before Antiochus Epiphanes had taken the extreme measures which provoked the Maccabaean revolt in 168 B.C., some of the priestly families had been uneasy about what was happening in Jerusalem and particularly in the Temple. A group of them had withdrawn altogether from participation in the Temple services, claiming as their justification the saying 'Oh that there were one among you that would shut the doors, that ye might not kindle fire on mine altar in vain!' (Mal. 1: 10). These men must have been even more deeply shocked and offended by what Antiochus Epiphanes did: they would be still far from satisfied with the way the restoration was carried out under Judas Maccabaeus. Some of these Hasidaeans, probably having been drawn somewhat reluctantly into armed resistance, withdrew altogether from Jerusalem, very probably when Alcimus was appointed as High Priest. They went into 'the land of Damascus', claiming that they were the true and faithful remnant of Israel entering into a new covenant. They looked forward to a time when they would gain control in the Temple and re-establish what they believed to be the proper priesthood and the proper rituals. They claimed that they themselves were the true Zadokite priesthood which had served in Jerusalem from the time of Solomon up to the time of Antiochus Epiphanes.

This may well be the society whose books have been found in caves near the Dead Sea. Their collection included not only copies of the books of the Old Testament and other religious works but also their own special books setting out their rules and customs and telling the story of their origins. Translations of these are available in a Pelican Book, *The Dead Sea Scrolls in English* by G. Vermès (Penguin Books, 1962). In telling the story of their beginnings they use the same kind of imagery as the author of Daniel did, though in the case of these scrolls the disguise is not so easy to penetrate. But it does seem quite clear that this society came into being because some Jewish priests thought it wrong to be associated at all with Jerusalem and the Temple as they were during the last two centuries before Christian times. Their headquarters was established at Qumran, on the north-west shore of the Dead Sea about five miles from Jericho; after a time their numbers increased and laymen were associated with them as well. There was a nucleus living in the central head-quarters and there were other groups associated with them in other parts of the country. It may be that at first they were in the north near to Damascus itself but at that period the Dead Sea district was under the same rule as Damascus and that may be why they described themselves as going to 'the land of Damascus'.

The sect was very strict. Members were bound to keep the Law of Moses according to the sect's interpretation and also to observe its very detailed community rules. At the festival of Pentecost they held an annual general assembly when new recruits were admitted and the progress of all members was reviewed. So they main-tained themselves as the true minority remnant, chosen by God to inherit the new covenant under the rule of the sons of Zadok. They are frequently described as the covenanters.

Although the documents which tell us about this group began to be discovered only in 1947 we did already know about the Essenes who were very highly thought of by Philo, the philosopher, and Josephus, the historian, who both wrote at the beginning of the Christian era. The Qumran group corresponds to a considerable extent with what these writers say about the Essenes and there is obviously a close relationship between them. The whole fellowship must have been a complex of very varied groups; some at the centre, some scattered about; some in towns, some avoiding the towns. All of them were claiming to be members of the true Israel and looking for the time when they would rule in Jerusalem and control the Temple and the life of the people.

The covenanters resisted the general trends of Judaism by withdrawing altogether from Jerusalem to keep themselves pure. The Pharisees resisted by developing their own special interpretations of the Law and keeping themselves separate from their neighbours. The Sadducees in power in the Temple and claiming the Zadokite priestly authority, were regarded by these other groups as unfaithful to the Law and the Covenant.

THE ROMANS, THE SELEUCIDS AND THE JEWS

The power and influence of Rome had been steadily growing and was now beginning to move eastwards. The Romans saw Judas Maccabaeus as a threat to Seleucid power and Judas saw Rome as a power to which he might well apply for help against Demetrius, who had supplanted Antiochus V in 162 B.C. Demetrius was a son of Seleucus IV who escaped from Rome and came to Syria to claim his father's kingdom. Judas's enemies, including the High Priest Alcimus, looked to Demetrius for help and support. But Judas's position was secured by his loyalty to the greater power of Rome.

Although Judas was killed in battle at Elasa in 160 B.C., the resistance was carried on after his death by his brothers, first Jonathan and then Simon. Their fight for power was successful, partly because of their skill in exploiting the decline of the Seleucid power, partly because of their nationalistic fervour. In 152 B.C. Jonathan took over the office of High Priest at the Feast of Tabernacles. This he was able to do because he was powerful enough to have got access to the necessary official garments. This High

Priest, though not of the right pedigree, was perhaps preferable to the traitorous hellenizer Alcimus, even though Alcimus was technically the legitimate High Priest. This is typical of the impossible choices with which Jews were faced in these extremely unsettled times: a High Priest powerful and loyal to Judaism but not qualified according to the Law to be High Priest, or a High Priest who was qualified for the office but disloyal to the Law? In fact these changes took place quite out of the control of the ordinary Jews and it must have been extremely confusing and frustrating and difficult for them to know where they stood. Jonathan was sufficiently secure in his position in Jerusalem to embark on capturing other cities, the neighbouring Greek cities; but eventually he was taken prisoner in Ptolemais and put to death in 143 B.C.

His brother Simon took his place immediately and in this year, 143 B.C., 'the people began to write in their instruments and contracts, In the first year of Simon the great high priest and captain and leader of the Jews' (1 Macc. 13: 42). The last of the hellenizers holding out in the Jerusalem citadel were removed in the following year. Other cities did not suffer the same bitter struggles between Judaism and Hellenism. In Alexandria and elsewhere fruitful contacts between the two worlds of thought were made which were very valuable for the future. In the New Testament books we see the results of these but also of the bitter struggles which took place in Jerusalem: if we may judge from Josephus, there were more struggles of this kind in many cities in the period around A.D. 70.

JERUSALEM INDEPENDENT

The Seleucid kingdom was threatened not only by the Romans in the west but also by the Parthians in the east. Demetrius went to fight on the eastern front in 139 B.C. and was taken prisoner. This left Simon free to bring order and security and further to extend the area of his rule. 'He made peace in the land, and Israel rejoiced with great joy: and they sat each man under his vine and his fig tree, and there was none to make them afraid' (1 Macc. 14: 11, 12). And he was a faithful Jew. 'The law he searched out, and every lawless and wicked person he took away. He glorified the sanctuary, and the vessels of the temple he multiplied' (1 Macc. 14: 14 b, 15).

Jerusalem could now again be recognized as the holy city to which Jews from all parts of the world looked, and to whose Temple funds they made financial contributions. Judaism in the dispersion, though it looked to Jerusalem as its focal point, differed in many respects from Judaism in Jerusalem and Judaea. There were settlements of Jews, some of long standing, in Egypt, which was still ruled by the Ptolemies, in the west under Roman rule, in the east under Parthian rule. Generally speaking these groups were well thought of by their fellow-citizens. They were industrious and reliable people and were sufficiently respected by others for their special religious views to be accepted. They earned some privileges and even a certain degree of serious interest in their beliefs and practices. This is illustrated by the letter of Aristeas, written in the second century B.C. by a very orthodox Jewish writer. He is writing as though he were a gentile explaining the Jews to Ptolemy Philadelphus (285–246 B.C.). He says, 'the God who gave them their law is the

God who maintains your kingdom. They worship the same God—the Lord and Creator of the Universe, as all other men, as we ourselves, O King, though we call him by different names such as Zeus or Dis.' But the Jews in Jerusalem and Judaea under Antiochus IV had not taken this view and their relations with gentiles (non-Jews) were consequently different.

After 129 B.C. the declining Seleucid power counted for nothing. For the Romans this meant that there was no defence between them and the Parthians; Palestine was their frontier but they did not immediately organize its defence. The high tone of the era of Simon Maccabaeus was not kept up by his successor as High Priest, John Hyrcanus, who was in power from 134 B.C. to 104 B.C., nor by Aristobulus I who actually styled himself king, nor by Alexander Jannaeus who reigned from 103 B.C. to 76 B.C. In about fifty years these Hasmonaean rulers extended their frontiers to approximately those of king David. In so doing they took control over very mixed groups of people who had been subjected to the full force of hellenizing policies and in many ways had benefited very much from them. Judaism was forced upon these people as a religion: yet from the point of view of the strict Jew this was a ludicrous and a sacrilegious impossibility: and from the point of view of, for instance, the Idumaeans it was an imposition. Idumaea is the hellenized form of the name Edom, familiar in the Old Testament, peopled by hereditary enemies of Israel, as the Jacob–Esau stories testify.

So it came about that in a sense Judaism was much more widespread in Palestine, but this Judaism bore little relation to the Law to which Jews in Jerusalem and many others widely spread around the world were so deeply devoted. The country to the north of the Israelite country is called 'Galilee of the nations' in the book of Isaiah (9: 1). This passage is quoted in Matthew and is translated as 'heathen Galilee' (4: 15). The phrase just means a foreign area, but the word 'Galilee' has come to be its proper name and this is another district which was forcibly brought under Jerusalem's jurisdiction and had Jewish Law imposed upon it. Relations with Jerusalem were not too cordial and scribes 'from Jerusalem' would perhaps not always be very welcome. John Hyrcanus destroyed the rival Samaritan temple on Mount Gerizim and it was never rebuilt, although the site remained a holy one and the Samaritans killed their Passover lambs there.

The policies and methods of these later Hasmonaean rulers were crude and cruel. Jews whose hopes for the nation were built on religious faith must have been aghast at the ways and means by which national power was being built up. Those who were well versed in the teachings of the prophets of the past must have seen history repeating itself and have feared that these new disloyalties would be punished by new disasters. There is a dilemma here which recurs very frequently. When things are going badly for Israel there will be some who say that this is the challenge to the People of God which they are called upon to resist in his name. There will be those who say that the bad times are the result of, or God's punishment for, Israel's disloyalty to the worship of Yahweh alone. There will be those who find either of these explanations inadequate and oversimplified. These different ways of interpreting the signs of the times lead to different ideas about what the People of God should be doing. These differences lie behind many of the conflicts within Judaism in New Testament times.

THE DECLINE OF THE HASMONAEANS

We have seen that the descendants of Mattathias and his patriotic sons became a quasi-royal family, involved in feuds and jealousies and struggles for power. Their effective power declined as did that of the Seleucid family and the way this worked out also left its mark on the Judaism of New Testament times.

Alexander Jannaeus got into serious trouble with the Pharisees. There is a story that once at the Feast of Tabernacles, just as he was about to perform the sacrifice, they shouted out that he was unfit for his office, certainly unfit to perform the sacrifice, and pelted him with fruit. For this they were brutally punished. But he seems to have realized that he had gone too far, and at the end of his life he advised his wife Alexandra to try to get their support. After his death Alexandra was queen, and one of her sons was High Priest.

Two sons of Alexander and Alexandra were involved at this time. The older was called Hyrcanus and as High Priest is known as Hyrcanus II. He seems to have been lacking in energy, Josephus tells us, and willing to conform to the demands of the Pharisees. The younger son was called Aristobulus and was a very different character. Before his mother's death he had taken control, and to this the lethargic Hyrcanus raised no objection. Alexandra's reign lasted from 75 B.C. to 66 B.C.

At this point another character appears from outside the family, Antipater, the governor of Idumaea. Idumaea was by now under Hasmonaean control, albeit reluctantly, and the Idumaeans had had Jewish Law imposed upon them. Antipater was a very able and very forceful person and he was determined to get control of Judaea, not by force but by subtler means. He had already established contact with the neighbouring kingdom in the south-east, Nabataea, with its capital at Petra. Antipater attached himself as a friend to the weak High Priest Hyrcanus II and in 67 B.C. persuaded Aretas, the Nabataean king, to march with an army to Jerusalem to support Hyrcanus in opposition to the stronger brother Aristobulus. The Nabataean forces were too strong for Aristobulus, and many of his supporters went over to his brother's side. Aristobulus himself and his closer associates withdrew to the Temple hill and Aretas besieged them there. In 63 B.C. Pompey the Great, later the rival of Julius Caesar, who had been entrusted by the senate of Rome with the task of securing the Parthian frontier, appeared in Jerusalem. Both sides in the conflict appealed to him for support, he ordered the Nabataeans home, and they went. Aristobulus, however, still held the Temple hill against the Romans for another three months. The arrival of Pompey, the end of both Seleucid and Hasmonaean power, was a milestone in the history of Judaea.

THE ROMAN OCCUPATION

Pompey abolished the Jewish kingdom and Aristobulus was sent captive to Rome. Pompey insisted on going into the Temple, including the Holy of Holies. He did not rob or damage the Temple, although he did not respect the Jewish scruples about holy ground. But otherwise he left the Temple and its services undisturbed and he re-established the mild Hyrcanus as High Priest. The Romans had already established Syria as a province; Palestine was now included under this head. Many of the cities which had been drawn into Jewish control in the heyday of Hasmonaean expansion came directly under Roman control and no longer owed any allegiance to Jerusalem. Yet, widespread as was the Roman empire, the boundaries of Judaism were wider still. In Parthia Jews were living who were descended from those taken captive to Babylon five hundred years before.

Antipater's plans for capturing Jerusalem had been foiled by Pompey's arrival at the critical moment. He did not abandon his ambition but waited for another opportunity and meanwhile made sure of his position in Roman favour. In 54 B.C. Crassus, the Roman governor of Syria, found himself in need of money for a military expedition against the Parthians. For this purpose he raided Temple funds. In the following year the Parthians defeated the Romans at the battle of Carrhae and this meant that the Roman frontier in Syria was severely threatened. Rome was also suffering from internal troubles and civil war. In 48 B.C. Pompey was defeated at Pharsalus by Julius Caesar and was murdered in Egypt shortly afterwards.

Antipater was not slow to offer his services to Caesar and brought to his assistance an army of Jews and Nabataeans. When Pompey had first come to Jerusalem and reinstated Hyrcanus II, he had sent his brother, Aristobulus II, to Rome: he and his sons Antigonus and Alexander had been there ever since and when Caesar wanted to harass Pompey he had released these three. At the time of Pompey's death Aristobulus and Alexander were both already dead, but Antigonus was alive and demanded of Caesar the position which his father Aristobulus had held in Judaea. Caesar decided against Antigonus in favour of Hyrcanus II. Antipater had always planned to use Hyrcanus as an instrument for his own ends and this brought him virtually to the position he had been working for. Antipater was given Roman citizenship and appointed as administrator in Judaea with authority to rebuild the walls of Jerusalem. When Caesar left, Antipater took charge and Hyrcanus II raised no objection to these arrangements.

Julius Caesar was murdered in 44 B.C. and yet another change of masters was to overtake the Roman world, including Syria. The struggle between Caesar's heir Octavian and his enemies Brutus and Cassius was fought out in the east. Octavian, with Antony, was victorious at Philippi in 42 B.C. and Antony moved eastwards when Octavian returned to Rome. A year before this, Antipater had been murdered and his sons Phasael and Herod had stepped into his place. Antony appointed these two to be tetrarchs (tetrarch means strictly a ruler over a fourth part but was used more generally) and left Hyrcanus as High Priest with his title of ethnarch (ethnarch means a ruler over a people and implies greater authority than tetrarch). Deputations of Jews begged to be rid of this family but their petitions were not heard. Antony moved on to Egypt.

In 40 B.C. the Parthians took their opportunity and invaded Roman Syria. Hyrcanus was removed from office and replaced by Antigonus, the man who had unsuccessfully applied to Caesar for the kingship. Phasael was killed but Herod escaped and made his way to Rome where he presented himself to Antony. It was arranged that the senate should appoint Herod as king: he was on the Roman side against the Parthians and would fight Antigonus who had turned out to be the enemy of Rome.

Herod set about making his title a reality. He landed at

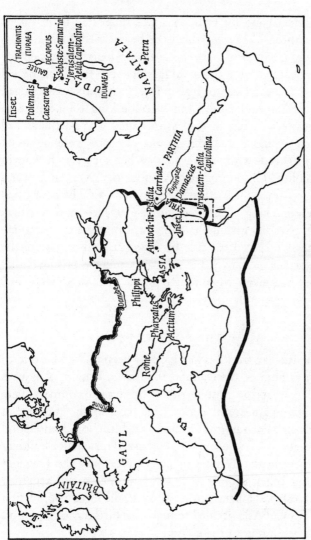

Fig. 3. The period of Roman supremacy.

Inset
TRACHONITIS
ITURAEA
GALILEE
DECAPOLIS
Ptolemais
Sebaste-Samaria
Caesarea
Jerusalem-
Aelia Capitolina
JUDAEA
IDUMAEA
NABATAEA
Petra

PARTHIA
Antioch-in-Pisidia
Carrhae
Euphrates
SYRIA
Damascus
Inset Jerusalem-Aelia
Capitolina
ASIA
Philippi
Pharsalus
Rome
Actium
Danube
Rhine
GAUL
BRITAIN

43

Ptolemais and for two years was supported from Egypt by Antony. During this time he married Mariamne, a granddaughter of Aristobulus II. By marrying a member of what had been the royal Hasmonaean family he hoped to please the Hasmonaean party. Jerusalem was besieged and taken and Herod thus became king of the Jews in Jerusalem in fact as well as in name. The Parthians had been repulsed and the Roman leaders were again at loggerheads with one another. When Octavian had again established his supremacy by his victory over Antony and Cleopatra at the battle of Actium in 31 B.C., he confirmed Herod as king of the Jews and he gave him more territory to govern, including Samaria. In 27 B.C. Octavian Caesar received the title of Augustus and in 20 B.C. the Parthians gave back the standards and the prisoners that they had taken when they overran Syria in 40 B.C.

THE ROMAN PEACE

The Roman frontiers had by now been pushed far out, to the Euphrates, the Danube, the Rhine, Britain. Augustus ruled over this vast territory through a comparatively stable and peaceful period. The end of the fighting in Palestine encouraged Herod to establish both himself and the city of Jerusalem and he embarked on a major building project in the Temple precinct. Not only the Jews but many other peoples welcomed the peace and regarded Augustus as a benefactor. In 9 B.C. the Greek population of Roman Asia decided to make the birthday of Augustus the beginning of the civil new year, saying:

Whereas the Providence which has ordered the whole of our life, showing concern and zeal, has ordained the most perfect consummation for human life by giving to it Augustus, by filling him with virtue for doing the work of a benefactor among men, and by sending in him, as it were, a saviour for us and those who come after us, to make war to cease, and to create order everywhere; and whereas Caesar, when he was made manifest, has caused the hopes of those who cherished anticipations (to be outstripped by what he has actually done), inasmuch as he has not only gone beyond previous benefactors, but has also left no hope to his successors of going beyond him; and whereas the birthday of the god (Augustus) was the beginning for the world of the glad tidings that have come through him... (From a decree of the Greeks of the province of Asia, *circa* 9 B.C., quoted from E. Barker, *From Alexander to Constantine*, Oxford, 1959).

Augustus deliberately restored much ancient Roman religious practice: hence it was quite natural that temples should be erected in many places dedicated to 'Rome and Augustus'; it was done by Herod in Palestine. So the birthday that the Asians celebrated with such enthusiasm was the birthday of a god. For the Jews who were devoted and committed to the worship of the one true God this kind of thing was impossible, embarrassing, absurd. They therefore offered prayer and sacrifice not *to* the emperor, but for him and on his behalf. While Augustus revived ancient Roman religion, he recognized that the Jews too had a valuable religion and were seriously devoted to it. Philo, the great Jewish philosopher of Alexandria, tells us that Augustus 'ordered that for all time continuous sacrifices of whole burnt offerings should be carried out every day at his own expense as a tribute to the most high God'.

Not only in Jerusalem where the Temple was but all over the empire Augustus respected the Jewish communities. This empire-wide body was numerous as well as unique. Philo tells us

So populous are the Jews that no one country can hold them, and therefore they settle in very many of the most prosperous countries in Europe and Asia both in the islands and on the mainland, and while they hold the Holy City where stands the sacred Temple of the most high God to be their mother city, yet those which are theirs by inheritance from their fathers, grandfathers and even ancestors farther back, are in each case accounted by them to be their fatherland in which they were born and reared, while to some of them they have come at the time of their foundation as immigrants to the satisfaction of the founders.

In the dispersion Augustus reaffirmed the permissions for synagogues and sabbath observance and the export of money to Jerusalem for the Temple tax. He restored some of the ancient Roman religious practice but the old gods of the Greek world could no longer command respect and intelligent Greeks had ceased to take them seriously. Many who did take human living and its responsibilities seriously were attracted to the Jewish religion and some became proselytes. Besides these full converts there were others who learned about Jewish beliefs and the Jewish way of life and were to be found in many synagogues. In Acts 13: 16 we read that Paul addressed the company in the synagogue at Pisidian Antioch as 'Men of Israel and you who worship our God' and later, in verse 26, as 'My brothers, you who come of the stock of Abraham, and others among you who revere our God'.

Augustus died in A.D. 14. During his time there was born in Palestine a boy named John who later came to be known by Christians as 'the Baptist' and a boy named Jesus who was known as 'of Nazareth'. This Jesus was

46

believed by many to be the Messiah and so came to be called Christ. Later generations judged his coming to have been of such significance that they decided to adopt a calendar which would make a fresh beginning there. So it is that when we study the reign of the great Augustus this new era begins within his lifetime. Luke tells us that Jesus was actually born at a time when 'a decree was issued by the Emperor Augustus for a general registration throughout the Roman world' (Luke 2: 1). But the local ruler in Palestine at this time was Herod and Luke begins his narrative with the words 'In the days of Herod king of Judaea' (Luke 1: 5); Matthew tells us Jesus was born 'during the reign of Herod' (Matt. 2: 1).

HEROD THE GREAT

Herod stood loyal to Augustus; he was enthusiastic about Greek culture, but realistic about Jewish religious fervour. After the long period of fighting there must have been a lot of restoration and rehabilitation to do: Herod had the resources and the determination to establish Jerusalem and Judaea very firmly. He built and rebuilt many cities. He rebuilt Samaria and called it Sebaste in honour of Augustus (Sebastos is the Greek for Augustus) and established a military colony there. This is the kind of place where Roman soldiers, left in Palestine after the struggle with the Parthians, would be settled. Although Greek was already a common language in these parts and the language of most leaders and officials was Greek, these soldiers would speak their own language of Latin. Herod also rebuilt Strato's Tower, an old Phoenician settlement which Alexander Jannaeus had captured, and called the new city Caesarea. This was a magnificent seaport and in it there was a magnificent temple to 'Rome and Augustus' and a statue of the emperor and one in honour of Rome.

The stability and prosperity of Jerusalem and Judaea depended considerably on the position of Jerusalem as the focal point of world-wide Judaism, a centre of loyalty and support. The Temple itself was maintained by considerable financial contributions from Jews all over the world. Herod realized how important it was that this should continue and also that the Jewish settlements should be well thought of in the cities where they were established. Because the Jews were privileged to export their money to Jerusalem for the Temple tax they did not pay full contributions into public funds because these funds paid the expenses of public worship, and Jews would not contribute to the worship of other gods either by their presence or by their money. Herod negotiated for confirmation of the privileges and better understanding of the position of the Jews in Asia.

In spite of all this it could not be expected that Herod could be popular at home. His means of coming to power and of retaining it were dubious and of course it was out of the question that Herod could be High Priest: he realized that it would be madness to try that. But he took authority to appoint the High Priest and not to regard this as a permanent appointment. So it came about that there were ex-High Priests, and these and their relatives were the group whom we find referred to in the New Testament as 'the chief priests'. Herod also had his own fortress in Jerusalem, called Antonia, from which he controlled the new Temple. He kept control over the High Priest by keeping the official robes in the fortress, for the High Priest could not officiate without them. Herod's buildings in Jerusalem, the theatre and the gymnasium, put Jerusalem into the class of beautiful cities of the hellenistic style though the Jewish Temple in its new magnificence still dominated it. 'Look, Master, what huge stones! What fine buildings!' (Mark 13:1). But the new customs associated with the gymnasium and theatre were deeply resented by the Jews to whom they were not only strange but shocking.

The central area of the Temple, including the Holy of Holies, took only eighteen months to complete. The second court was surrounded by a balustrade which had slabs built into it on which it was stated that no foreigner might enter the Holy Place. The prohibition was stated in Latin and in Greek. The other buildings and outer courts were under construction for many years; in fact the Temple was not completed until long after Herod's death. In spite of Herod's reputation as a brutal tyrant it was impossible not to admire this beautiful building. 'It has taken forty-six years to build this temple. Are you going to raise it again in three days?' (John 2:20). No wonder the people were bewildered by Jesus's challenge, 'Destroy this temple' (John 2:19). But over the great gate a great golden eagle was erected. To the Jews this was an image, and a particularly offensive one, for it was the Roman emblem. A party of indignant Jewish students, encouraged and supported by their teachers, attacked this eagle with hatchets. They did it openly as an aggressive protest and about forty were arrested. Those actually caught in the act were burnt alive.

Herod had been made king of the Jews by the senate in Rome. At the end of his life when he was old and ill there must have been anxiety and speculation about his successor. The members of his numerous family were immediately concerned for he had married many wives. So were the populace of Jerusalem, wondering what the future might hold, and the Pharisees and the Sadducees with their own particular concerns and ambitions. If 'astrologers from the east arrived in Jerusalem, asking, "Where is the child who is born to be king of the Jews?"' (Matt. 2: 1b, 2), it is not surprising that 'King Herod was greatly perturbed when he heard this; and so was the whole of Jerusalem' (Matt. 2: 3).

Herod had a number of descendants, none on very good terms with one another or with him. His first wife, Doris, he dismissed and later on also her son Antipater. He married Mariamne, a Hasmonaean, with a view to fathering Hasmonaean princes. But Herod's sister, Salome, poisoned his mind against Mariamne and in 29 B.C. she was executed; there were two sons of the marriage, Alexander and Aristobulus, and they were sent to Rome for their education. In 18 B.C. Herod paid a state visit to Augustus and when that was over he took the young men back with him. Aristobulus was married to his cousin Berenice, Salome's daughter, and Alexander to the daughter of the king of Cappadocia. The two brothers were soon informed that their father had murdered their mother, Mariamne, and a family feud started. Herod had ten wives, so there must have been many cross-currents of jealousy and hatred. Things got so bad that in 12 B.C. Augustus tried to reconcile this divided family; he succeeded, but only for a short time. Herod recalled Antipater, Doris's son, and made him and Alexander and Aristobulus his heirs. But all these three were dead before Herod. When the last of the three, Antipater, was executed in 4 B.C. Herod made a new will, in favour of Archelaus, son of Malthace, his Samaritan wife.

The date of Herod's death was the year 4 B.C. This appears strange, as Jesus was already born in Herod's lifetime. Some centuries after the decision had been taken to measure a new era from the time of the birth of Jesus and to count the years as A.D. (anno domini means in the year of the Lord), some modifications had to be made in the calendar and this date is one of the strange results. Jesus was born a few years before Herod died and was a young man of about twenty when Augustus died.

HEROD'S SUCCESSORS

Herod had in his will declared that his son Archelaus was to succeed him. Archelaus knew this and he took charge accordingly. He also knew that his appointment was subject to confirmation from Rome. Even before Archelaus set out for Rome to press his claims the resentment which had smouldered against his father Herod broke out.

There was trouble at Passover in 4 B.C. when numbers of pilgrims were in Jerusalem for the feast. Archelaus's punishments were cruel and the people went home angry. On the next festival occasion, Pentecost, only seven weeks later, the numbers of pilgrims coming to Jerusalem were swollen by many who were determined to secure justice. This was a bid for full independence, an attempt to turn the Romans out of Jerusalem by force and Sabinus, Roman governor in Syria, was hard pressed. Varus the legate, the emperor's representative in command of the army, came himself from Antioch with two legions; the attackers dispersed and when he entered Jerusalem the residents asserted that they had had no responsibility for the disorders but had been unable to restrain the others.

A party of fifty Jews had already set out for Rome, with

Varus's permission, after the death of Herod and before the revolt began. They wanted a measure of freedom, that is to say rule by the High Priest and Sanhedrin, the highest Jewish court, directly responsible to the Roman legate in Syria. Full freedom and independence were obviously out of reach but this arrangement would release them from the immediate rule of a semi-foreign Herod or of a foreign procurator. This party was probably composed of Pharisees and Sadducees, typical of the majority of the Jerusalem population who had not been active in the revolt.

Archelaus set out for Rome, but at Caesarea he met Sabinus on his way to take charge until the emperor's decision should be known. Varus, the legate, came too to Caesarea. Everyone must have been nervous about what might happen. Varus let Archelaus and his party go on to Rome and prevented Sabinus from going to Jerusalem. He left a legion there to keep order and himself returned to Antioch. Another section of the Herod family also went to Rome with Archelaus's brother Antipas, to support his claim to be appointed king of the Jews. When they all reached Rome it was obvious that all of them would really prefer to be directly under the administration of a Roman governor but that if they had to have a member of the Herod family as king they would all prefer that it should be Antipas. So it was agreed that they would all accuse Archelaus of having exceeded his authority by the severity of his punishment of the rioters in Jerusalem. The case for Antipas was drawn up by Salome, Herod's sister, who had been involved in these intrigues for so long, and before the rival claimants were summoned to the imperial council both cases were presented to Augustus in writing.

Date	Events	Herods	Governors of Judaea	Roman Emperors	New Testament Writings
10 B.C.	Birth of Jesus	Herod the Great (37-4 B.C.)		Augustus (27 B.C.: A.D.14)	
A.D.		Archelaus (4 B.C.-A.D.6)			
10		Philip the Tetrarch (4 B.C.-A.D.34)	Coponius (6-9) Marcus Ambivius (9-12) Annius Rufus (12-15)		
20		Herod Antipas (4 B.C.-A.D.39)	Valerius Gratus (15-26)	Tiberius (14-37)	
30	Ministry of John the Baptist Ministry of Jesus Crucifixion & Resurrection Paul's Conversion		Pontius Pilate (26-36)		
40		Herod Agrippa I (37-44)	Marcellus (36-37) Marullus (37-41)	Gaius Caligula (37-41)	
50	Paul's first journey Council of Jerusalem Paul's second journey Paul's third journey	Herod Agrippa II (50-53)	Cuspius Fadus (44-46) Tiberius Alexander (46-48) Cumanus (48-52) Felix (52-60)	Claudius (41-54)	1 & 2 Thessalonians 1 & 2 Corinthians Galatians
60	Paul's arrest Paul's voyage to Rome Paul's martyrdom		Festus (60-62) Albinus (62-64) Gessius Florus (64-66)	Nero (54-68)	Romans Philippians Colossians Philemon Mark
70	Destruction of Jerusalem Temple vessels to temple of Peace in Rome			Galba (68-69) Otho (69) Vitellius (69) Vespasian (69-79)	
80				Titus (79-81)	Matthew Luke Acts
90				Domitian (81-96)	Revelation
100				Nerva (96) Trajan (98-117)	John
110					
120					
130	Building of Aelia Capitolina began on site of Jerusalem Revolt under Bar-Cochba crushed				

Fig. 4. A time chart of the New Testament.

From the Roman point of view the best thing would have been to go on with the previous arrangement, if only any of the candidates had shown evidence of suitability for the job. None of them, however, had the combination of qualities and characteristics which had earned for their father the title of 'Great' nor could any of them be relied upon to serve Roman purposes on the Parthian frontier as he had done. This is what is reflected in the decision which was made. Archelaus was given half the kingdom, Jerusalem, Judaea, Idumaea and Samaria, with the title of ethnarch and the promise that he should be made king if he proved himself. The other half was divided into two tetrarchies: one was given to Antipas, who had claimed the throne, and the other to Philip, yet another son of Herod, who had been sent to Rome by Varus. Antipas ruled Peraea and Galilee, an awkward territory divided by the Decapolis area. Philip had a district north-east of the sea of Galilee. Otherwise the members of the family received the sums of money willed to them by Herod.

Archelaus did not earn his promotion. Far otherwise, he ruled so badly that Augustus gave way in A.D. 6 when Jews and Samaritans together, in spite of their distrust for one another, petitioned for his removal. Yet Archelaus could surely not have survived in power for as long as ten years if there had not still been powerful men who had supported Herod and his family and wished their rule to go on. Herodian partisans sided with Jesus's opponents (Mark 3: 6; 12: 13). In the New Testament we read that Joseph was afraid to go to Judaea when he heard that Archelaus had succeeded his father Herod there (Matt. 2: 22). Archelaus was tried in Rome and exiled to Gaul and his share of his father's kingdom became a Roman province to be known as 'Judaea'. The two tetrarchs, Antipas and Philip, and their tetrarchies remained undisturbed for nearly thirty years.

JUDAEA UNDER ROMAN GOVERNMENT

In A.D. 6 Judaea was put under direct Roman control, as some of the Jews had asked in 4 B.C. This country was still virtually the eastern frontier of the Roman empire and therefore strategically very important. Judaea was ruled by a series of governors whose Roman title was *praefecti* and from the reign of Claudius (A.D. 41) *procuratores*. The best known of these is Pontius Pilate who is described as 'the Roman Governor' (Matt. 27: 2) and 'governor of Judaea' (Luke 3: 1). Jerusalem was the centre of the widespread and increasingly powerful Jewish people and it was important to Rome from that point of view too. The Jews now had no king; their only head was the High Priest. Successive High Priests were appointed by the Romans but this did not prevent the office from increasing in prestige and in symbolic significance; particularly was this true for the Judaism of the dispersion. The Temple and the Temple tax and the synagogues and the sacred books all enjoyed Roman protection and the High Priest was the key figure in the pattern.

Within the limitations of being ruled by a foreign power this arrangement was acceptable to the Sadducees and High Priestly groups. Such power as the Jews had was in their hands and naturally they were anxious not to lose it. If disorder threatened they were naturally afraid lest 'the Romans will come and sweep away our temple and our nation' (John 11: 48). The Pharisees, however, were not happy about being subjected to foreign rule and although they too were anxious that the nation should be preserved they thought that the ruling party might be paying too high a price for this in their collaboration. There were others who shared these doubts, including those still loyal to the house of Herod. 'Master, you are an honest man, we know, and truckle to no man, whoever he may be; you teach in all honesty the way of life that God requires. Are we or are we not permitted to pay taxes to the Roman Emperor? Shall we pay or not?' (Mark 12: 14, 15 a). As for the covenanters (p. 33), they looked for the day when they would overthrow the present Temple group. They believed that nothing could go right for Israel until they themselves were in control. There were Zealots too whose name explains itself, patriots hoping to regain Jewish independence by the use of force.

Many of these different groups were looking, as the Israelite prophets had so frequently looked in the past, for signs of the beginning of the end. Some looked for a leader who would be a descendant of the great king David, the Lord's anointed, who would lead them to victory. It was for the kingdom of God that they all waited, passively or actively but all earnestly. Simeon was 'upright and devout, one who watched and waited for the restoration of Israel' (Luke 2: 25) and Anna talked about the child Jesus 'to all who were looking for the liberation of Jerusalem' (Luke 2: 38).

Considering all this Jewish ferment, everything went remarkably smoothly under the Roman governors. They were generally efficient and responsible officers, but things were not so happy under Pontius Pilate, whose term of office began in A.D. 26. It was in his time that 'John the Baptist appeared in the wilderness' and 'His proclamation ran: "After me comes one who is mightier than I"'

(Mark 1: 4, 7). John attracted attention because of the way his prophetic message fulfilled the words of Isaiah, 'Prepare a way for the Lord; clear a straight path for him' (Matt. 3: 3). Both Pharisees and Sadducees were looking for signs to indicate that Israel's great day might be at hand; and a prophet of the old kind would indeed be such a sign. Both Pharisees and Sadducees came to hear John, much as they disagreed with one another on so many matters of belief and policy. He preached repentance, to be demonstrated by acceptance of baptism, the cleansing rite, and when he saw Pharisees and Sadducees coming for baptism he warned them, 'Then prove your repentance by the fruit it bears; and do not presume to say to yourselves, "We have Abraham for our father"' (Matt. 3: 8, 9). Even the Jew with the surest and purest pedigree, descent from Abraham, must repent and receive forgiveness for his sins if he is to be fully prepared for the great Day.

Also during the time of Pontius Pilate, Jesus, who had preached both in Judaea and Samaria and also in Galilee where Herod Antipas still ruled, and who was believed by many to be the mightier one of whom John had spoken, was crucified. Leaders of all the Jewish parties decided that he was a danger to the position of all of them and of Roman authority itself. Pontius Pilate seems to have been suspicious of their motives, and doubtful of the justice of their charge against him. The Jews said, 'If you let this man go, you are no friend to Caesar; any man who claims to be a king is defying Caesar' (John 19: 12). 'Then at last, to satisfy them, he handed Jesus over to be crucified' (John 19: 16). On the cross the charge against the criminal was posted up. It was written in Hebrew, Latin, and Greek. And it said 'King of the Jews'. It was a terrible warning to all, for here was publicly proclaimed the fate of any who challenged Caesar. But although the Jews themselves had brought this charge, the inscription looked somewhat insulting to them as well and they asked Pilate to change it, but he would not.

HEROD ANTIPAS

Both John the Baptist and Jesus of Nazareth spent time in Galilee and Peraea, the territory ruled by Herod (i.e. Antipas). It was Herod, in fact, who was responsible for the imprisonment and execution of John. When Jesus's ministry was making a stir in Galilee 'Prince Herod heard of all that was happening, and did not know what to make of it; for some were saying that John had been raised from the dead, others that Elijah had appeared, others again that one of the old prophets had come back to life. Herod said, "As for John, I beheaded him myself; but who is this I hear such talk about?"' (Luke 9: 7–9). Herod would be well aware of the significance of such talk and the possible threat to his own position as well as to the Roman government on which ultimately he depended for that position.

When, later on, Jesus in his turn had been arrested in Jerusalem at the time of Passover, Herod was in the city too. So when Pilate heard that Jesus was a Galilean he remitted the case to Herod. 'When Herod saw Jesus he was greatly pleased; having heard about him, he had long been wanting to see him....Herod and his troops treated him with contempt and ridicule, and sent him back to Pilate dressed in a gorgeous robe. That same day Herod and Pilate became friends: till then there had been a standing feud between them' (Luke 23: 8–12). At this juncture their anxieties and fears were the same and so too their relief when this new and puzzling threat was removed, as they thought, when Jesus was put to death.

Herod's brother, Philip the tetrarch, died in A.D. 34. The emperor Tiberius appointed no successor to him but added his territory, Ituraea and Trachonitis, to the province of Syria. Four years later Herod's nephew, Agrippa I, arrived to take up the kingship of what had been Philip's tetrarchy. This had been given to him by the new emperor Gaius, sometimes known by his nickname Caligula. Herod went to Rome to request the same title for himself but Gaius sent Herod into exile and added his territory to Agrippa's kingdom.

THREATS TO THE TEMPLE

Pontius Pilate was not very sensitive to the religious scruples of the Jews. He secretly brought into Jerusalem the military standards which he described as being 'effigies of Caesar'. The Jews protested strongly and Pilate attempted to enforce his intentions, but when he was faced with a body of Jews inviting death rather than submission to this sacrilege he withdrew. He was removed from office in A.D. 36. Vitellius, the legate, appointed a new High Priest and gave the High Priest's garments back into Jewish care. This might have been the beginning of renewed mutual confidence but unfortunately the new emperor destroyed any such hopes. For twenty years no emperor had forced the issue with the Jews about the ruler-cult. But just as Antiochus Epiphanes had disastrously done this two hundred years before, so did Gaius in A.D. 37.

Tiberius died in A.D. 37. He was succeeded by Gaius who was emperor for four years, and was assassinated in

A.D. 41. Gaius gave orders that statues of himself were to be set up in the Jewish sanctuary at Jerusalem. In the event of trouble the Jews responsible were to be put to death and the whole people reduced to slavery. The legate of Syria, now Petronius, did his best with unwelcome orders. He reasoned with the Jews that all other subject nations had erected statues of Caesar. The Jews appealed to their Law, which was supposed to enjoy Roman protection, and Petronius pointed out to them that he was under orders. The Jews were adamant and Petronius withdrew. When Gaius received his report of what had happened he ordered Petronius to kill himself, but Petronius had heard the news that Gaius had been murdered before this message reached him.

There was also anti-Jewish feeling in Alexandria at this time. Representatives of Jews and Greeks from that city were in Rome early in the reign of Gaius putting their respective cases before him. There was a long history of disharmony in Alexandria and Philo tells us that Jewish indignation was further roused by the threat to erect a statue of the emperor himself in the Jerusalem Temple. When Gaius was assassinated the immediate danger to peace was averted: a threat to Jerusalem was a threat to Jews everywhere and had Gaius's plans and orders been carried out there might have been widespread trouble.

THE ROMANS, THE JEWS AND THE CHRISTIANS

Claudius, the new emperor, appointed Agrippa to be king over the whole kingdom which his grandfather Herod the Great had ruled, including Judaea and Samaria, and some additional territory besides. Agrippa was descended from Herod and Mariamne the Hasmonaean. He was on good terms therefore with the Jews in Judaea as well as with important people in Rome where he had been brought up. But when he died in A.D. 44 (Acts 12) no comparable successor was available: his son was too young and Judaea was again put under Roman governors.

By now there was a new factor in the Jewish situation. Jesus of Nazareth had been crucified as a danger to peace, and now his followers were claiming that God had raised him from death and that he really was the Messiah. This new group threatened to be a new danger. Felix, who was governor in Judaea from A.D. 52 to A.D. 60 was faced with a problem in Jerusalem; the commandant there discovered that the Jew Paul, one of this group, whom he rescued first from the mob and then from a plot to kill him, was a Roman citizen and could therefore expect protection. 'A great uproar broke out...and the commandant was afraid that Paul would be torn in pieces, so he ordered the troops to go down, pull him out of the crowd, and bring him into the barracks' (Acts 23:9, 10). After he had been told about the plot he issued orders to 'Get ready two hundred infantry to proceed to Caesarea. ...Provide also mounts for Paul so that he may ride through under safe escort to Felix the Governor' (Acts 23:23, 24). Some of his fellow-Jews described Paul as 'a perfect pest, a fomenter of discord among the Jews all over the world, a ringleader of the sect of the Nazarenes' (Acts 24:5). Felix 'happened to be well informed about the Christian movement' (Acts 24:22). He kept Paul in safety at Caesarea and left him still in custody, when, after two years, he was succeeded by another governor, Festus, in A.D. 60.

The Jewish leaders were equally unsuccessful with Festus in their plans to be rid of Paul. Paul refused

Festus's proposal that he should once more return to Jerusalem for his case to be heard there. He appealed to Caesar. 'Then Festus, after conferring with his advisers, replied, "You have appealed to Caesar: to Caesar you shall go"' (Acts 25: 12). And so Paul eventually went to Rome, in custody, where now Nero was emperor, having succeeded Claudius in A.D. 54. Nero blamed the Christians for the great fire which broke out in Rome in A.D. 64 and he put many of them to death.

In Palestine relations deteriorated again under later governors and nothing could dissuade the Jews from breaking out into violent resistance. In A.D. 66 Eleazar, son of the High Priest, persuaded the Temple officials to reject the sacrificial offerings brought on behalf of Rome and the emperor. The resistance was determined and once more there were ardent nationalists who hoped that God might intervene to restore the kingdom to Israel; meanwhile they set about trying to recover it themselves. The revolt was sufficiently serious for a general, Vespasian, to be sent from Rome to Judaea and he came in A.D. 67, but Jerusalem is a difficult city to capture and the campaign was interrupted because Nero died and Vespasian became emperor. It was not until A.D. 70, when Titus renewed the siege of Jerusalem, that the rebellious Jews were defeated. The city was destroyed, including the magnificent Temple so recently completed, and Jews throughout the world suffered in the loss of their great Temple and centre. In Titus's triumphal procession in Rome were carried some of the Temple vessels and a copy of the Jewish Law. These, as they may still be seen in Rome, portrayed in the arch of Titus, demonstrated the Roman victory in the Jewish war, the end of this threat to the Roman peace. But it was not the end of Judaism, nor of the Law.

THE NEW TESTAMENT

When Vespasian completed the temple of Peace in Rome in A.D. 75 the Temple vessels from Jerusalem were put into it, and he kept the copy of the Law in his own house. But Judaism survived the destruction of the Temple and still throughout the empire the Law was studied and observed. The Christians also were widespread by now, sometimes still associated with the Jewish groups, in some places already estranged from them. Their particular beliefs and their unique message emphasized a new beginning, a New Covenant already in operation. Over a period of forty years this group had grown in spite of some strong opposition and when Vespasian took the Jewish Law home with him after Titus's triumph, Paul's letters which later came to be included in the books of the New Testament had already been written. Most of the material used in preaching and teaching was still handed on orally but by this time some of the other leaders of the movement may have written down some of it and their work may have been used by later writers in the books we now have in the New Testament.

While Judaism was learning to live without the focal point of the Jerusalem Temple and while Christianity was learning its world-wide vocation there were still small groups of Jews in Palestine trying to resist the Romans. In A.D. 130 orders were given for the building of a Roman town to be called Aelia Capitolina on the site of Jerusalem. This led to open revolt under Bar-Cochba, lasting for three years and only finally put down in A.D. 135. By this time all the books of the New Testament had probably been written but they had not even yet all been collected together.

3

HOW THE NEW TESTAMENT CAME INTO BEING

In the second letter to Timothy in the New Testament (2 Tim. 4: 13) you may read the following request: 'When you come, bring the cloak I left with Carpus at Troas, and the books, above all my notebooks.' What were these books and notebooks that this writer was so anxious to get back, together with his warm wrap for the winter? One thing is clear; they did not include what we call the New Testament. It is difficult for us to picture any body of Christians without that book; but there had been Christians for something like a hundred years, before its separate parts had even all been written, let alone gathered together into the collection which is now known as 'the New Testament'.

As a matter of fact, the actual title 'the New Testament' did not begin to be used for this collection of Christian writings until round about A.D. 300. But the title implies something which had long before then become evident—that these books contain the story of God's new 'testament', that is, his new 'covenant' or 'agreement' with his people—the continuation and renewal and crown of the 'old covenant' made through Moses with Israel. In Jer. 31: 31 the prophet looks forward to the new covenant that God was going to make, to meet the situation caused by the breaking of the old covenant. The writings of the New Testament contain the story of the fulfilment

64

of the prophet's hopes. And just as these Christian writings were called the New Testament, the pre-Christian Jewish writings eventually came to be called, by Christians, the Old Testament.

Substantial parts of what was thus to become the New Testament, such as the Gospel and Letters of John and the Revelation, were probably not completed until about A.D. 100, when there had already been Christians for some 70 years. 2 Peter may be even later; and more time still went by before these writings began to be collected together. Therefore, the writings already mentioned by the author of 2 Timothy cannot have included the New Testament as such. 'The books' in that verse are likely to have been scrolls containing the Jewish scriptures—which, as has just been said, Christians today generally call the Old Testament—and 'the notebooks' may have contained jottings by the writer himself.

So here is a reminder that the body we call 'the Church'—that is, Christians everywhere—set out on its long journey with no distinctively Christian books. Neither, for that matter, had it any buildings of its own. There was 'the Church'—that is, all Christians—but there were no churches—that is, special buildings for Christian worship. Neither were there at first any professional, full-time ministers; still less did schools or universities have the Christian religion in their syllabus.

THE CHRISTIAN BOOKS SPRANG FROM THE CHURCH'S WORK AND LIFE

Until all this is grasped, it is impossible to begin to understand how the New Testament, as we now call it, came to be written and collected and accepted. It grew up after the Christian Church itself had been launched, and its different books were the result of all sorts of different situations and crises and needs. The Christian writings grew out of the heart of a living, witnessing, suffering, worshipping companionship of ordinary people. In these writings we can hear their cries and prayers, their praises and their arguments. In the same way, it was out of the actual needs and circumstances of people that there sprang the final decision about which books were to be treated as authoritative, that is, recognized by the Church as a whole as carrying weight.

Naturally, each writer had a great deal to do with the shaping and arranging and phrasing of his own writing; but we shall get the whole picture out of proportion if we lose sight of the communities to which these individual persons belonged and of which they were mouthpieces. We have to remember the needs and plans and intentions of each whole community, as it tried to find and follow God's will. It was the community's needs that led to the moment when at last an individual picked up a pen and actually set the words down in writing.

THE CHURCH AS WITNESS RATHER THAN AS TEACHER

The early Christians, remember, were, for the most part, not learned people or scholars. As Jews—and the earliest were all Jews—they had probably all learned to read and write in some village school, organized in connexion with the local Jewish place of worship, the synagogue. As children they would have been taught here to read and learn by heart the Jewish scriptures, either in the original Hebrew or, in some synagogues, translated into Aramaic or Greek, just as devout Muslims today are trained on the Quran, the sacred book of Islam. And they had, no doubt, learnt the numerals and could do arithmetic. Thus they were literate—indeed, within certain limits, well educated; but certainly they were not scholars nor in most cases learned in the literature of Greece and Rome. They did not face the world as teachers, they had no new ideology or philosophy. They had a new life, but no new theory of life or system of ethics. The one distinctive thing about them was their witness to Jesus as the 'King' of God's choice—or, to use the Jewish terms, the 'Christ' or 'Messiah', that is, the one whom God had chosen to be ceremonially anointed as king. They knew about his life and teaching, they were convinced that, though he had certainly been put to death, he had been seen and heard again after this, by good witnesses. This same Jesus had been seen and met with, truly alive; and they believed that in him God's plan for the world, of which their Jewish scriptures spoke, had reached its climax. In this sense, the scriptures had been 'fulfilled', and Jesus of Nazareth had turned out to be the centre of the pattern of fulfilment: he was the coping-stone of the building, the meaning of all that God had been doing in his dealings with his People from the very beginning.

These convictions were visibly expressed among the Christians by two things. First, there was baptism 'into the name of Jesus'; that is, the person to be admitted into the Christian Church was plunged in water, or had water poured over him, as a symbol of his acceptance of Jesus as Lord and of his belonging to Jesus Christ, crucified and raised to life again. This was done once and for all. Then, secondly, came the repeated communal meal at which bread and wine were associated with the death and resurrection of Jesus Christ; and with it came a strikingly new quality of fellowship. This is how the newly formed Christian community is described in Acts 2: 42 ff.:

They met constantly to hear the apostles teach, and to share the common life, to break bread, and to pray. A sense of awe was everywhere, and many marvels and signs were brought about through the apostles. All whose faith had drawn them together held everything in common: they would sell their property and possessions and make a general distribution as the need of each required. With one mind they kept up their daily attendance at the temple, and, breaking bread in private houses, shared their meals with unaffected joy, as they praised God and enjoyed the favour of the whole people. And day by day the Lord added to their number those whom he was saving.

Of course, that picture drawn by the author of the Acts must not mislead us into imagining that the early Christians everywhere simply knocked off work and spent all their days in religious exercises. The situation in Jerusalem was, in any case, not typical. In the first place (Acts 2: 1–11), a considerable proportion here was probably made up of Jewish pilgrims from elsewhere who had come to keep the festival of Pentecost, so called because it fell on the fiftieth day (in Greek, *pentecoste*) after a certain day in the preceding festival of Passover. These pilgrims, drawn into the Christian Church, had then stayed on, away from their homes and their normal occupations. And secondly, it is likely that they expected a dramatic climax—the return of Christ—very shortly, and this, too, made them less ready to return to settled occupations. We may be sure that elsewhere, after a short time, Christians were to be found faithfully pursuing their ordinary occupations as traders, shopkeepers, and so on.

But, even if the Acts picture is not absolutely representative, it nevertheless throws into relief the distinctive
marks of the Christian Church wherever it may be: the
apostles' teaching about Jesus and the resurrection; the
communal life, in which each member has a concern and
responsibility for the others; and, at its centre, the Christian sacraments of Baptism and Holy Communion,
Eucharist or Lord's Supper.

THE APOSTLES' PROCLAMATION

The apostles' teaching: what, precisely, was this? Probably there was nothing that more decisively moulded
Christian writing than this pattern of apostolic preaching.

If you look back in Acts 2 to the passage which leads
up to what has just been quoted, you will see the explanation of their existence offered by these followers of Jesus
of Nazareth, these Nazarenes, as they were called. Notice,
incidentally, that they were not yet called Christians.
That began later, at Antioch in Syria—see Acts 11: 26;
and then it seems to have been not the Christians' own
choice of name, but a mocking nickname given by non-
Christians. Their explanation of themselves, spoken in
the passage in Acts 2 by Peter, ran something like this:

(i) the plan of God, as reflected in the Jewish scriptures,
has reached its climax, its critical moment (Acts 2: 16–21);

(ii) Jesus of Nazareth, a man who had recently lived
among them, had been attended wherever he went by
exceptional signs of God's power and presence (verse 22);

(iii) the Jews had handed him over to the gentiles and
had him cruelly executed, fastened up on a wooden cross
and left to die (verse 23);

(iv) but even this turned out to be under God's control

69

and used by him as part of his design; and God had raised him from death and vindicated him as more than merely a man—as Lord (verses 23–36).

That was the explanation, in outline; and then followed its application:

(v) if you admit all this, and accept Jesus as Lord, then you must change your attitude; you must submit to the rite of baptism: you must be plunged in water while declaring your acceptance of Jesus as Lord. This is a mark and a means of coming penitently to belong to Jesus Christ and of being forgiven; and then you will receive this new power of God's presence which is beginning to show itself among his people (verse 38).

That, in outline, is what the apostles proclaimed, and how they drove it home and applied it when it had made its impact on the hearers. You will notice two very important things about it. The first is that items (i) to (iv) are not mere exhortation to be good, but statements. You may or may not believe them, but they are statements: grammatically speaking, they are in the indicative mood —not exhortations in the subjunctive or commands in the imperative. They do not moralize or reprove or plead or command: they just state or declare. That is why New Testament scholars make much of the Greek word *kerygma*, which means a herald's announcement. *Kerygma*, proclamation or announcement, well sums up this 'indicative' quality of the Christian good news. It is only *after* the statement that the appeal or exhortation comes (no. v); and the second point is that, even then, it is not an appeal to be good, or to try to be like Jesus, or to improve one's morals. It is an appeal to 'belong'—to be, by baptism, made a part of the People of God.

Many people think of the Christian message as a pious

summons to be good; but according to the specimen we are examining it is a plain statement—'Here is a God who has shown that he can give you the power to live a full and true life'—followed by an appeal—'Let yourself be joined to him!' This involves penitence—acknowledging God's goodness and admitting where we have gone wrong; trust—relying on God as he shows himself to us in Jesus Christ; and loyalty—responding to him with our undivided affection and energies.

THE GOSPELS: WHAT ARE THEY?

This statement which the Christians offered is repeated, one way and another, in other parts of the Acts and elsewhere in the New Testament, and forms the structure underlying the Gospels. Here is one more instance from the Acts:

You know about Jesus of Nazareth, how God anointed him with the Holy Spirit and with power. He went about doing good and healing all who were oppressed by the devil, for God was with him. And we can bear witness to all that he did in the Jewish country-side and in Jerusalem. He was put to death by hanging on a gibbet; but God raised him to life on the third day, and allowed him to appear, not to the whole people, but to witnesses whom God had chosen in advance— to us, who ate and drank with him after he rose from the dead. He commanded us to proclaim him to the people, and affirm that he is the one who has been designated by God as judge of the living and the dead. It is to him that all the prophets testify, declaring that everyone who trusts in him receives forgiveness of sins through his name (Acts 10: 38–43).

'Gospel' is an Anglo-Saxon word for good news. 'Evangel', which is also sometimes used, is from the

Greek word for good news, *euangelion*. An evangelist is thus one who writes a Gospel or who preaches the gospel; and it is precisely because our Gospels contain essentially this same statement of good news that they are so named. They are about Jesus as the fulfiller of God's design in the Jewish scriptures, as one accompanied by exceptional signs of God's presence, as crucified, and as raised from death.

The Gospels tell the same story as is contained in the apostles' proclamation, examined on pp. 69 f. The Gospels of Matthew, Mark, and Luke, at any rate—we shall come to John later—are not primarily exhortation any more than the sermons in the Acts are. Like the sermons, they are primarily statement. What mainly distinguishes them from the proclamation of the Acts is that they all three contain actual anecdotes to illustrate what is barely alluded to in Acts 10. They give actual examples of how Jesus went about helping those who were in need, and of what wonderful and extraordinary cures he worked. They describe what led up to the clash with the Jewish authorities; and they also, especially Matthew and Luke, contain a great deal of Jesus's own teaching, which scarcely appears in the sermons in the Acts. But they are not 'lives' of Jesus or biography in the ordinary sense: they do not describe what Jesus looked like or give a connected story of his life. Instead, they press home, by anecdote and illustration, the apostles' witness and the apostles' view of who Jesus was and how he stands as the very coping-stone of the building which God had designed from eternity.

In other words, the figure of Jesus and his teaching, as they are presented in the Gospels, concern the kingdom of God, that is, God's reign over his world. The reign of

God is the theme of the Gospels. But Matthew, Mark, and Luke—John, again, is rather different—do not go on to the apostolic exhortation, 'be baptized! be incorporated!' This was an exhortation which could not be given, in any distinctively Christian setting, until after the death and resurrection of Jesus; and these Gospels although written after these events, represent, in the main, the message about what led up to them, not what followed and sprang from them. It is true, of course, that the fully Christian response to the message, is, in a sense, anticipated even in the story of Jesus. Every disciple who follows him is, to that extent, responding to his challenge. But this is still not the same as entry into membership of the Christian Church. Broadly speaking, Matthew, Mark, and Luke represent items (i) to (iv) in the analysis on pp. 69 f. above, but stop short of (v).

THE SYNOPTIC GOSPELS AND
THE ACTS OF THE APOSTLES

The adjective 'synoptic'—derived from Greek *syn*, 'together', and a verb-root connected with 'seeing'—is applied to Matthew, Mark, and Luke as the three Gospels which follow the same general pattern and can therefore be arranged in parallel columns in a 'synopsis', and seen together.

But while it is true that all three of these Gospels follow broadly the pattern of the apostles' proclamation, each of them sprang from a particular situation and has its particular plan and purpose and its special features.

(a) Mark

In about A.D. 320, Eusebius, bishop of Caesarea, wrote in Greek a history of the Church. Eusebius reports that

Papias, who was bishop of Hierapolis, in Asia Minor, in about A.D. 130, had recorded a tradition that Mark's Gospel was a translation into Greek of the teaching which the apostle Peter had given in Rome. Peter himself presumably used Aramaic, a language similar to Hebrew. It is generally assumed that the Mark who wrote the Gospel was the young man called John Mark in the Acts (12: 12, 25; 15: 37, 39), who was indeed a companion of the apostles. This identification is not absolutely certain—Marcus was a common name—and how far this Gospel depends upon traditions associated with Peter has been questioned. But parts of it do, in fact, read like a direct, eyewitness account; and a recently discovered copy of what seems to be a genuine letter of Clement of Alexandria (about A.D. 190), also speaks definitely of Peter's notes as forming part of Mark's material.

It is very widely believed to be earlier than Matthew or Luke, but much hard thinking about this question is still going on, and rather startling new ideas may yet emerge. On any showing, however, Mark's Gospel is separated from the events it describes by, at most, a generation—perhaps less. Peter was martyred round about A.D. 60. Even if the Gospel was put together after that, it is not much later. At latest, it was probably written not more than some thirty to thirty-five years after the death of Jesus; and the traditions it draws on take us, in some cases, right back to the very words of Jesus himself.

Thus, we may say with confidence that Mark is at least a very early example—and possibly the first ever to exist—of an arrangement into a connected whole of the traditions previously circulating as separate units, whether spoken or written. It is one of our earliest examples—if not the earliest—of the piecing together of separate units

74

of written and oral tradition into a continuous whole, with the apostles' proclamation as its framework.

It presents its brief anecdotes with impressive directness and simplicity and swiftness. Without any preliminary account of Jesus's birth and childhood, it dives straight into the story by introducing John the Baptist and recounting how Jesus came to him for baptism. Then, in quick succession, specimens are given of what Jesus did and said, of how the crowds responded but the religious leaders resented him, and of how he trained his small band of close friends and followers. About two-fifths of the whole book are devoted to the closing days of his life; and then the narrative breaks off abruptly at the empty tomb. What follows (16: 9 ff.) is a summary of the traditions about the subsequent events. It is generally recognized that this is a later addition, patched on by some other writer; but it was early enough, even so, to get into the Gospel in its accepted form.

Thus Mark is a little handbook for basic Christian instruction, simple, yet brilliantly dramatic—a stark, powerful presentation of the Christian facts: not a biography, but a portrait of Jesus as the spokesman and bringer of the kingdom of God, and as far more than a martyr—as the triumphant and victorious Son of God. It was probably written for the leader of some Christian community, to help him in teaching his people. It may well have been some time before there were enough copies of it to distribute to the leaders of other communities— and longer still before there were enough for individuals to possess one for themselves. Remember, a book had to be laboriously copied out by hand, and papyrus, the paper of those days, was not always easy to obtain in quantity.

(b) Matthew

But, sooner or later, Mark evidently came to be copied and sent round and widely known and read outside the circle for which it was first written; and Matthew seems, to most scholars, to be based on Mark. There is a great deal of additional material in Matthew, and the writer has followed an arrangement of his own; but very little of Mark's material is omitted, even though it is rewritten. The word 'rewritten' is here used on purpose, because careful examination suggests that, where Matthew gives the same material in different words, he is often using Mark as his source and rewriting it so as to improve the style or condense it or otherwise adapt it to his own purposes.

There is much uncertainty about the origin and circumstances of this Gospel; but its character and contents suggest that it was written to help Christians to understand the origins of their faith and to defend and explain themselves before non-Christian Jews. Its material is very skilfully arranged, for the most part in great sections such as the 'Sermon on the Mount' (chapters 5–7), or the collection of parables in chapter 13. It contains a great deal more of the teaching of Jesus than Mark does, and it is even more explicit about the fulfilment of Old Testament prophecy. It seems to be a handbook of instruction for Church leaders as they trained their people to understand and defend their convictions.

How the additional material reached the writer can only be guessed at: it probably represents converging streams of tradition flowing through several different channels, and worked in by him in his rewriting of Mark. As for Mark, so for Matthew, Eusebius quotes Papias's opinion. Papias said that the apostle Matthew wrote the *logia*, that is 'sayings', in Hebrew—he probably means Aramaic—and that these were translated in various ways. This implies that as we have it in Greek Matthew is a direct translation of something actually written by an apostle. It is now, however, generally agreed that our Matthew is not simply a translation of an Aramaic Gospel. There may well have been an original apostolic document in Aramaic: Papias's tradition is hard to explain if it does not contain a core of truth. But our Greek Gospel was evidently put together by someone who could write his own Greek, however much he may have copied and transcribed and even translated bits and pieces of tradition that had reached him from earlier days. It is impossible to say who that someone was. His character and gifts can only be guessed at, if at all, by studying those parts of the Gospel which seem most obviously to be the work of his own editorial hand.

(c) *Luke–Acts*

Luke and Acts both open with a dedication to someone named Theophilus, and, in the Acts, there is an explicit reference back to 'the first part of my work'. Thus the two clearly belong together, and there is every reason to believe the early tradition, appearing in various places, notably a very old prologue to Luke's Gospel, that both the books are by Luke. Luke is actually mentioned as a companion of Paul in Col. 4: 14 (where he is called a doctor), in Philem. 24, and in 2 Tim. 4: 11. Moreover, there are sections of Acts where the writer says 'we' did so-and-so. These are: Acts 16: 10–17, where they left Asia Minor and crossed over to Europe, and went to Philippi; 20: 5 — 21: 18, where Paul left Greece and went to Jerusalem; and 27: 1 — 28: 16, the journey to Rome, with shipwreck on the way. These 'we-sections' confirm the idea that the author was a fellow-traveller of Paul's.

Luke, like Matthew, evidently used Mark's Gospel. A great deal of its other (non-Marcan) material is similar to or identical with material in Matthew. This has led to the conclusion that among the sources used by both Matthew and Luke was not only Mark but also some other source generally labelled 'Q' by modern scholars. It is not certain who first gave it this label, or why. The fact that the German for 'source' is *Quelle* is not necessarily the reason. But more important than the origin of the label is the nature of this source. Perhaps the best theory is that 'Q' was the Aramaic collection of *logia* or 'sayings' of Jesus which Papias said the apostle Matthew had written. Of course, it is possible to think of other explanations for the sharing of the same material by Matthew and Luke—for instance, that Luke copied from Matthew or Matthew from Luke, and that Mark is not a source but an abridgement of Matthew. But Mark shows quite independent signs of being earlier than Luke and Matthew. This makes it most likely that it is one of the sources of them both; and Matthew and Luke are so different in their arrangement and manner that it is not easy to believe that one copied from the other. So the 'two-document hypothesis'—that Matthew and Luke both used Mark and 'Q'—remains a strong one.

But each has, in addition, material all his own. Matthew's 'Sermon on the Mount' contains much that can be found scattered over Luke, but more besides. Matthew has other teaching and parables found in no other Gospel, and a great many stories, such as that of

Peter walking on the water, and Pilate's wife's dream, and Judas's death. Luke, similarly, contains whole sections which have no parallel in Matthew. The long section Luke 9: 51 — 18: 14 contains a particularly large amount of material found in no other Gospel, such as the sending out of the seventy messengers, and the stories of the good Samaritan, the two sons (commonly called 'the Prodigal Son'), the dishonest bailiff, the rich man and the beggar, the Pharisee and the tax-collector. It looks, therefore, as though there were special traditions lying behind Matthew and Luke respectively—very likely from different centres: possibly Antioch for Matthew, and Caesarea for Luke, but these are only guesses.

To return to Luke–Acts, it looks as though the author had in fact carried out the intentions he expresses in the first words of his Gospel and of the Acts—to write a connected account of the story of Jesus and its sequel. He evidently sees the story in clearly marked stages or phases. The birth of John the Baptist, with which he starts, is itself the climax of the long story of the Jewish people—the story of the Old Testament. Then comes the ministry of Jesus, with his death, resurrection, and ascension as its climax. There follows the era of the missionary expansion of the Christian Church, with the arrival of Paul in Rome as its climax. Each stage or phase closes with something that leads on to the next; the reader is given a most vivid sense that God is in control of the whole sequence; and the writer has an exceptional gift for drawing word-pictures which sum up and represent important aspects of the whole story. Here is Jesus in the synagogue in his own town of Nazareth, fulfilling all God's plans for his people, yet blindly rejected by them and resented:

At these words the whole congregation were infuriated. They leapt up, threw him out of the town, and took him to the brow of the hill on which it was built, meaning to hurl him over the edge. But he walked straight through them all, and went away (Luke 4: 28–30 (see verses 16–27)).

Or here is the group of the friends of Jesus enabled by the Holy Spirit to make their witness understood by all the nations of the world:

Now there were living in Jerusalem devout Jews drawn from every nation under heaven; and at this sound the crowd gathered, all bewildered because each one heard the apostles talking in his own language. They were amazed and in their astonishment exclaimed, 'Why, they are all Galileans, are they not, these men who are speaking? How is it then that we hear them, each of us in his own native language? Parthians, Medes, Elamites; inhabitants of Mesopotamia, of Judaea and Cappadocia, of Pontus and Asia, of Phrygia and Pamphylia, of Egypt and the districts of Libya around Cyrene; visitors from Rome, both Jews and proselytes, Cretans and Arabs, we hear them telling in our own tongues the great things God has done' (Acts 2: 5–11).

Or again, the Jerusalem church meets in conference to make the momentous decision, reached only after pro-longed debate, that non-Jews may be admitted to the community without the Jewish rite of circumcision:

It is the decision of the Holy Spirit, and our decision, to lay no further burden upon you beyond these essentials: you are to abstain from meat that has been offered to idols, from blood, from anything that has been strangled, and from fornication. If you keep yourselves free from these things you will be doing right. Farewell (Acts 15: 28 f. (see verses 6–27)).

Or here is Paul, in Rome at last, still in conflict with his unbelieving fellow-Jews:

...he spoke urgently of the kingdom of God and sought to convince them about Jesus by appealing to the Law of Moses and the prophets. This went on from dawn to dusk (Acts 28: 23 (see verses 17–31)).

Luke–Acts is a series of incidents, chosen so as to portray vividly the essential steps and stages by which Israel—the People of God of the Old Testament—finds its true fulfilment in the Christian Church, despite the refusal of non-Christian Jews to recognize 'the Nazarenes' as true Israel. It also shows, again and again, how the Christians were supported by the Roman government: it is as much as to say, 'You Romans have really always been on the Christian side'. Possibly 'his Excellency Theophilus' (Luke 1: 3) was a Roman official.

THE GOSPEL ACCORDING TO JOHN AND
THE LETTERS OF JOHN

This Gospel is distinguished from the other three in many ways. For example, it is not 'synoptic' (see p. 73), it cannot be arranged successfully in a fourth column side by side with the other three: its pattern is different and it does not share the sources which they seem to share in common. It contains no stories of 'exorcisms', that is, of the cure of people possessed by 'demons'. The supreme miracle of the resurrection is, of course, shared by all the Gospels. The only other specific miracle stories that John shares with the rest are the wonderful feeding of the great crowd, and the walking on the water afterwards; other-wise it has its own special stories. The Gospel is largely concerned with Judaea and Jerusalem, whereas the others give more space to Galilee, except, indeed, in their long closing sections dealing with the end of Jesus's ministry—

which was, of course, according to all of them, in Judaea. It represents Jesus as speaking and teaching in ways which are not exactly paralleled in the synoptic Gospels: instead of parables and terse, pointed sayings, there are comparatively long, connected discourses and arguments, and one or two examples of the kind of picture-language which is best called 'allegory' rather than 'parable'. In other words, there is a contrast between, for instance, the parables of the synoptic Gospels—parables such as those of the tiny mustard-seed that grows into a big plant, or of the almost invisible yeast that makes a great lump of dough rise—and the meditations which John gives us in the form of allegories about the shepherd and the sheep or the vine and the branches.

A difference which is still more striking and more far-reaching than these is that, in John's Gospel, Jesus makes explicit claims for himself which, in the other Gospels, are for the most part only hinted at or implied; and he is represented as doing this from the very beginning of his ministry. And, with this, there go allusions to the spiritual union between Christians and Christ which are lacking in the synoptic Gospels. In other words, in these Gospels Jesus is reserved about his own status, and describes the relationship of others to him simply in terms of discipleship, but the Jesus of the fourth Gospel speaks already like the Lord his friends discovered him to be after the resurrection. Already he answers the question 'What must I do to be saved?' 'Everyone who drinks this water'—ordinary, literal water—'will be thirsty again, but whoever drinks the water that I shall give him will never suffer thirst any more. The water that I shall give him will be an inner spring always welling up for eternal life' (John 4: 13 f.); '...it is my Father's will that

everyone who looks upon the Son and puts his faith in
him shall possess eternal life; and I will raise him up on
the last day' (John 6: 40); 'I am the vine, and you the
branches. He who dwells in me, as I dwell in him, bears
much fruit...' (John 15: 5).

It is this highly developed, reflective quality of John's
Gospel which chiefly led to the view that it must be a
comparatively late writing, far removed from the actual
story of the life of Jesus of Nazareth, and written, perhaps, by some dreamer who, with little contact with the
actual history, spun out of his own imagination a picture
of the Jesus he had come to know in mystical experience.
But the facts are not so simple as that. In the first place,
the evangelist himself insists most strenuously on the
reality of the physical events. It is he who sums up the
whole story in the phrase 'the Word'—that is, God's own
utterance—'became flesh' (John 1: 14), and he will not
ever allow the reader to detach himself from things and
places—from material, historical circumstances such as
Aenon near Salim, Jacob's well, the pool Bethesda, a hill-
side where there was plenty of grass, and so forth. Again,
prolonged study has led many to the conclusion that, if
not always, yet at least sometimes, John has more accurate
traditions than even the synoptic Gospels. Perhaps he
even knows a good deal about how disputes were con-
ducted in Judaea with the trained religious authorities.

In other words, it is most unlikely that this writer was
only using the form of a Gospel and the mere semblance
of a historical story in order to convey an independent
message of his own. Rather, he is using traditions about
Jesus—some of them apparently very early and historically
sound—and retelling them in such a way as to bring
home the conviction that the 'Jesus of history', the very

man who lived and suffered in the time of Pontius Pilate, was also and at the same time the divine Son of God, the Saviour of the world—the very one who, after his death and resurrection, was found to be 'the Lord of faith'. This writer, even more clearly than the authors of the other Gospels, writes history so as to make it transparent and luminous—so as to show us the depths beneath it and the infinite vista beyond it.

It is impossible to be certain whether or not the writer of this Gospel was actually the apostle John, writing in his old age and in the light of long experience of the risen Lord. But if it is some other—some disciple of his, perhaps—then at least, it appears, he is using traditions belonging to the eyewitness apostle himself. The Gospel may have been written in Ephesus, perhaps for Christians and non-Christians alike, and for Jews and gentiles alike. It possibly has a special message for that type of religious person later known as a gnostic. *Gnōsis* is simply the Greek for 'knowledge'; but the term (and the derived word 'gnostic', meaning 'concerned with *gnōsis*') has come to be used for a sort of religious speculation which stressed mystical union with God but had little or no concern for the material world or for history— least of all for 'the Word' becoming 'flesh'. John's Gospel uses some of the language of such mystical speculation but keeps the reader's feet firmly on the solid earth and insists on flesh and blood. It would be a splendid reply to this irresponsible sort of speculation. The same kind of speculation is still current now in what is called theosophy.

In sum, then, this writer drew his material from the same main event as the synoptic evangelists, but seems to have largely used a different group of traditions, and to have handled them in such a way as to bring out doctrinal convictions about the nature of Christ and the way of new life which the synoptic Gospels also imply, but refrain from making so explicit.

The three Letters of John evidently spring from the same circle of ideas, and use many of the same phrases. It is possible that they were addressed, later than the Gospel, by the same writer, to his friends, collectively and individually, when they were in danger of falling away from the great central convictions expressed in the Gospel.

THE LETTERS OF PAUL AND OTHERS

But it is time to go back from the writers of the Gospels, and meet some other writers. Within the New Testament, the Acts is the only narrative account of the Church; and, after chapter 12, even the Acts is largely the story of one man, Paul. But a great deal of light is thrown also by the letters of Paul and others and by the book called the Revelation (not 'Revelations' as it is often incorrectly called).

Paul was very likely the inventor of the particular type of letter which is now associated with him. We possess numberless non-Christian Greek letters from about the same period—scraps of papyrus, the paper of those days, preserved by chance in the hot, dry sands of Egypt, and ranging from the notes of businessmen driving hard bargains to affectionate or angry correspondence between parents and children, or letters of sympathy in bereavement. But among these there is nothing that can be compared to Paul's letters. They are, in the first place, very much longer than the average; and, then, consist almost entirely not of personal news and messages, which are kept down to the minimum, but of teaching and advice to his converts based on the most profound insight into the nature and meaning of the death and resurrection of Jesus Christ, and its consequences. These are genuine letters. They are addressed mainly to groups of Paul's personal friends, and they begin and end with special, Christian forms of the ordinary letter greetings, and contain brief, affectionate messages. But they are filled, from end to end, with practical, theological exposition of astonishing depth and magnificence. Instead of always writing with his own hand, Paul evidently made extensive use of his friends as secretaries, and a good deal of what we read may have been fairly freely written up by them: but his powerful thought, and often what are evidently his very own phrases, come irresistibly through this exciting, spirited, daring Greek. Paul's letters are among the most intoxicating parts of the whole New Testament. But he cannot have written them with the faintest notion that they would become 'scripture' or even be preserved for long. They are eager, hard-hitting letters, dealing with all sorts of different crises and problems among the communities of Christians which had been called into being by the apostle's words and witness, in the towns of Galatia (in Asia Minor), in Thessalonica, in Philippi, in Corinth, in Rome, and elsewhere.

Besides the letters bearing Paul's name, the New Testament contains several others. There is the anonymous one to Hebrews, sometimes wrongly attributed to Paul; the Letter of James, two attributed to Peter, three to John (already mentioned), and one to Jude. There is much discussion about the identity of the writers; also, in the case of some of these writings, it is a question whether they may not be treatises in letter-form rather than real letters. But, for all such discussions, reference must be made to the relevant commentaries.

CHRISTIAN LIFE AND THOUGHT REFLECTED
IN THE LETTERS

In these writings you can catch echoes of Christian evangelism and teaching, worship and sermons; you can witness some of the conflicts of race and class that tore the ancient world as they do our own; and you can watch the Christian gospel meeting these problems.

(a) *The proclamation of the gospel*

Many, at least, of these letters were written before even the earliest of the Gospels—probably Mark's, as has been argued above—came to be written; so it is all the more interesting to find clear reflexions of the apostolic pro-clamation, the *kerygma*, whose form is described on pp. 69 f., already visible:

And now, my brothers, I must remind you of the gospel that I preached to you; the gospel which you received, on which you have taken your stand, and which is now bringing you salvation. Do you still hold fast the Gospel as I preached it to you? If not, your conversion was in vain.

First and foremost, I handed on to you the facts which had been imparted to me: that Christ died for our sins, in accordance with the scriptures; that he was buried; that he was raised to life on the third day, according to the scriptures; and that he appeared to Cephas, and afterwards to the Twelve. Then he appeared to over five hundred of our brothers at once, most of whom are still alive, though some have died. Then he appeared to James, and afterwards to all the apostles.

In the end he appeared even to me; though this birth of mine was monstrous, for I had persecuted the church and am therefore inferior to all other apostles—indeed not fit to be called an apostle. However, by God's grace I am what I am, nor has his grace been given to me in vain; on the contrary, in my labours I have outdone them all—not I, indeed, but the grace of God working with me. But what matter, I or they? This is what we all proclaim, and this is what you believed (1 Cor. 15: 1–11).

More compressed and more theological is this, from the beginning of Romans:

From Paul, servant of Christ Jesus, apostle by God's call, set apart for the service of the Gospel.

This gospel God announced beforehand in sacred scriptures through his prophets. It is about his Son: on the human level he was born of David's stock, but on the level of the spirit—the Holy Spirit—he was declared Son of God by a mighty act in that he rose from the dead: it is about Jesus Christ our Lord. Through him I received the privilege of a commission in his name to lead to faith and obedience men in all nations, yourselves among them, you who have heard the call and belong to Jesus Christ (Rom. 1: 1–6).

There are many other passages besides which carry the stamp and pattern of the apostolic proclamation—for instance, it reappears very clearly in the pattern of Christian worship described in (c) below—but the two just quoted may serve as specimens.

(b) Teaching

But, once the gospel had been proclaimed and accepted, there followed 'teaching'—the explanations naturally called for by the inquirer or (if he had been baptized immediately after being converted) even by the baptized Christian. The Greek word for teaching is *didache*, and it is often used in discussions of the New Testament, in contrast to *kerygma*, 'preaching'. An inquirer would need not only to have a fuller version of the original proclamation, or *kerygma*, containing the kind of detail about

Jesus which later the Gospels were to offer, but also to be given teaching, or *didache*, about the conduct expected of Christians, about the right way to behave towards non-Christians, about how to regulate family life, how polygamy and pagan morals had to be dealt with, how slaves should regard their masters, how Christian masters should treat their slaves, and so on.

All this, too, Paul's letters reflect. Broadly speaking, each of these letters tends to fall into two parts—first the doctrinal part, which springs out of the original proclamation, and then the ethical part, which draws practical conclusions from the doctrine. Romans is a particularly clear example: Rom. 1–11 is doctrinal, 12–15 is ethical (16 is concerned mainly with personal messages). One can easily see that a Christian evangelist and teacher would be constantly using such material. A genius like Paul, no doubt, gave it a very special stamp of his own; but even so, his letters reflect the kind of thing that must have been constantly on the lips and in the minds of every pastor and leader. This is confirmed when one sees letters by other writers following similar lines. Thus, the teaching in Rom. 13: 1–7 is very much like that in 1 Pet. 2: 13–17. Here is Rom. 13: 1–7:

Every person must submit to the supreme authorities. There is no authority but by act of God, and the existing authorities are instituted by him; consequently anyone who rebels against authority is resisting a divine institution, and those who so resist have themselves to thank for the punishment they will receive. For government, a terror to crime, has no terrors for good behaviour. You wish to have no fear of the authorities? Then continue to do right and you will have their approval, for they are God's agents working for your good. But if you are doing wrong, then you will have cause to fear them; it is not for nothing that they hold the power of the sword, for they are God's agents of punishment, for retribution on the offender. That is why you are obliged to submit. It is an obligation imposed not merely by fear of retribution but by conscience. That is also why you pay taxes. The authorities are in God's service and to these duties they devote their energies.

Discharge your obligations to all men; pay tax and toll, reverence and respect, to those to whom they are due.

And here is 1 Pet. 2: 13–17:

Submit yourselves to every human institution for the sake of the Lord, whether to the sovereign as supreme, or to the governor as his deputy for the punishment of criminals and the commendation of those who do right. For it is the will of God that by your good conduct you should put ignorance and stupidity to silence.

Live as free men; not however as though your freedom were there to provide a screen for wrongdoing, but as slaves in God's service. Give due honour to everyone: love to the brotherhood, reverence to God, honour to the sovereign.

Again, compare Jas. 4: 6–10 with 1 Pet. 5: 5–9.

Jas. 4: 6–10:

Thus Scripture says, 'God opposes the arrogant and gives grace to the humble'. Be submissive then to God. Stand up to the devil and he will turn and run. Come close to God, and he will come close to you. Sinners, make your hands clean; you who are double-minded, see that your motives are pure. Be sorrowful, mourn and weep. Turn your laughter into mourning and your gaiety into gloom. Humble yourselves before God and he will lift you high.

1 Pet. 5: 5–9:

In the same way you younger men must be subordinate to your elders. Indeed, all of you should wrap yourselves in the garment of humility towards each other, because God sets his face against the arrogant but favours the humble. Humble yourselves then under God's mighty hand, and he will lift you up in due time. Cast all your cares on him, for you are his charge.

Awake! be on the alert! Your enemy the devil, like a roaring lion, prowls round looking for someone to devour. Stand up to him, firm in faith, and remember that your brother Christians are going through the same kinds of suffering while they are in the world.

Other parallels can easily be drawn. Teaching about masters and servants, for instance, is found in more than one of Paul's letters—see Col. 3: 22 ff. as one example—and also in 1 Pet. 2: 18 ff. But enough has been said to illustrate the way in which early Christian instruction can still be heard sounding through the New Testament letters.

(c) Worship

A great deal of the language in Paul's letters and elsewhere in the New Testament evidently echoes Christian worship.

Once or twice, indeed, it looks as though a Christian hymn were actually being quoted. Here are two examples:

And so the hymn says:
> 'Awake, sleeper,
> Rise from the dead,
> And Christ will shine upon you.' (Eph. 5: 14)

And great beyond all question is the mystery of our religion:
> 'He who was manifested in the body,
> vindicated in the spirit,
> seen by angels;
> who was proclaimed among the nations,
> believed in throughout the world,
> glorified in high heaven.' (1 Tim. 3: 16)

But, quite apart from passages like these, which seem to be actual quotations, it is clear that the language of praise and prayer shaped a good deal of the New Testament, and that it was through worship that some of the traditions about Jesus were handed down.

The most obvious example of such preservation of traditions in worship is, no doubt, the 'institution narrative' as it is called. In Mark 14: 17–31, and the parallels in Matt. 26 and Luke 22, there are accounts of what happened at the last meal shared by Jesus with his friends in the upper room in Jerusalem before he went out to his arrest and death, and of how he startlingly associated the bread and wine with his own body and blood. There is little doubt that, if not the whole story, at least these 'words of institution'—the words which 'instituted' the Lord's Supper (or 'Holy Communion' or 'Eucharist') and set it going as a regular rite to be continued by the disciples—were repeated, whenever Christians met to 'break bread' in the Lord's name. Thus Paul reminds his friends at Corinth of the solemn tradition he had received and passed on to them:

For the tradition which I handed on to you came to me from the Lord himself: that the Lord Jesus, on the night of his arrest, took bread and, after giving thanks to God, broke it and said: 'This is my body, which is for you; do this as a memorial of me.' In the same way, he took the cup after supper, and said: 'This cup is the new covenant sealed by my blood. Whenever you drink it, do this as a memorial of me.' For every time you eat this bread and drink the cup, you proclaim the death of the Lord, until he comes (1 Cor. 11: 23–6).

Again, one can overhear the unmistakable tones of worship and adoration in such passages as these: Eph. 1: 3f.:

Praise be to the God and Father of our Lord Jesus Christ, who has bestowed on us in Christ every spiritual blessing in the heavenly realms. In Christ he chose us before the world was founded, to be dedicated, to be without blemish in his sight, to be full of love. . . .

1 Pet. 1: 3:

Praise be to the God and Father of our Lord Jesus Christ, who in his mercy gave us new birth into a living hope by the resurrection of Jesus Christ from the dead!

In the Acts, to revert for a moment to that book, there is an instructive passage (Acts 4: 23–31), where one can actually watch the christianizing of Jewish forms of worship. In this instance, a Jewish type of address to God as Creator and a Psalm—Ps. 2—are woven together and given a distinctively Christian application:

As soon as they were discharged they went back to their friends and told them everything that the chief priests and elders had said. When they heard it, they raised their voices as one man and called upon God:

'Sovereign Lord, maker of heaven and earth and sea and of everything in them, who by the Holy Spirit, through the mouth of David thy servant, didst say,

'Why did the Gentiles rage and the peoples lay their plots in vain?

The kings of the earth took their stand and the rulers made common cause

Against the Lord and against his Messiah.'

They did indeed make common cause in this very city against thy holy servant Jesus whom thou didst anoint as Messiah. Herod and Pontius Pilate conspired with the Gentiles and peoples of Israel to do all the things which, under thy hand and by thy decree, were foreordained. And now, O Lord, mark their threats, and enable thy servants to speak thy word with all boldness. Stretch out thy hand to heal and cause signs and wonders to be done through the name of thy holy servant Jesus.'

When they had ended their prayer, the building where they were assembled rocked, and all were filled with the Holy Spirit and spoke the word of God with boldness (Acts 4: 23–31).

Exactly the same kind of thing can be seen happening in one of the early Christian writings not included in the New Testament, the so-called *Didache* or 'Teaching' of the Twelve Apostles (see p. 107).

But as touching the eucharistic thanksgiving give ye thanks thus. First, as regards the cup: We give thee thanks, O our Father, for the holy vine of thy servant David, which thou madest known unto us through thy servant Jesus: thine is the glory for ever and ever. Then as regards the broken bread: We give thee thanks, O our Father, for the life and knowledge which thou didst make known unto us through thy servant Jesus; thine is the glory for ever and ever. As this broken bread was scattered upon the mountains and being gathered together became one, so may thy Church be gathered together from the ends of the earth into thy kingdom; for thine is the glory and the power through Jesus Christ for ever and ever (*Didache* 9: 1–4).

Thus—to return to Paul's letters—such writings as these evidently echo the words which must often have been on the lips of Christian leaders as they led their people in worship. In 2 Cor. 1: 20 there is even an allusion to the actual Christian formula of prayer, 'through Christ Jesus', and the response, 'Amen':

[Jesus] is the Yes pronounced upon God's promises, every one of them. That is why, when we give glory to God, it is through Christ Jesus that we say 'Amen'.

There is a great deal, also, in the New Testament letters that seems to spring straight out of Christian baptism. The public baptism of an adult was a very dramatic thing: it was a kind of visible acting out of the gospel. The new convert faced the west, the region of sunset and darkness, and renounced the evil powers that had dominated his former life; then he took off his old clothes and was plunged down into the water in the name of Jesus; and then came up from it to receive, perhaps, anointing with oil or the laying on of hands which signified the gift of the Holy Spirit, and to be clothed with new clothes. Can we doubt that the pattern of this drama had shaped Paul's words when he wrote the following?

What are we to say, then? Shall we persist in sin, so that there may be all the more grace? No, no! We died to sin: how can we live in it any longer? Have you forgotten that when we were baptized into union with Christ Jesus we were baptized into his death? By baptism we were buried with him, and lay dead, in order that, as Christ was raised from the dead in the splendour of the Father, so also we might set our feet upon the new path of life (Rom. 6: 1–4);

—or this?

Did you not die with Christ and pass beyond reach of the elemental spirits of the world?...

Were you not raised to life with Christ? Then aspire to the realm above, where Christ is, seated at the right hand of God, and let your thoughts dwell on that higher realm, not on this earthly life. I repeat, you died; and now your life lies hidden with Christ in God. When Christ, who is our life, is manifested, then you too will be manifested with him in glory.

Then put to death those parts of you which belong to the earth—fornication, indecency, lust, foul cravings, and the ruthless greed which is nothing less than idolatry....

But now you yourselves must lay aside all anger, passion, malice, cursing, filthy talk—have done with them! Stop lying to one another, now that you have discarded the old nature with its deeds and have put on the new nature, which is being constantly renewed in the image of its Creator and brought to know God. There is no question here of Greek and Jew, circumcised and uncircumcised, barbarian, Scythian, freeman, slave; but Christ is all, and is in all.

Then put on the garments that suit God's chosen people, his own, his beloved: compassion, kindness, humility, gentleness, patience...(Col. 2: 20; 3: 1–5, 8–12).

As for 1 Peter, it has even been suggested that it is built up from the baptismal ceremony and sermon. Whether that is so or not, it is certainly full of baptismal language and ideas; 1 John also may be a kind of recall to baptism for believers who are in need of the strength and re-assurance of their original baptism, with its offer of God's help and its demand for man's loyal response.

(d) Sermons

If we turn to the more instructional side of worship, it is possible that in a connected argument like Rom. 9–11 we may see the line that Paul had often taken in sermons. By a 'sermon' is here meant not exactly the evangelist's *kerygma* or proclamation, nor yet the individual instruction given to an inquirer by his teacher, but rather a public piece of instruction or exhortation—what used to be called a homily.

It was some time before the Christians found themselves permanently excluded from the Jewish synagogues, and Paul must very often have preached in them. Synagogues were, as they still are, the local Jewish meeting-places in towns all over the world where, every sabbath (the period from sunset on Friday to sunset on Saturday), there was a meeting for worship and instruction. In Luke 4: 16ff. Jesus is described as preaching in the Nazareth synagogue. In Acts 13: 15 there is an account of how Paul and Barnabas, visiting a synagogue in a town called Pisidian Antioch (in Asia Minor) were, there and then, invited to give an extempore talk. (The synagogue authorities little anticipated the result!) Again, it has been conjectured that the Letter of James may be based on synagogue preaching. At any rate, whether in synagogues or at specifically Christian meetings elsewhere, there must have been Christian sermons or homilies. These, too, have left their mark on the New Testament literature—whether in connected argument about a specific subject, such as 'the Jewish problem', as in Rom. 9–11, or in passages of exhortation to Christian behaviour such as Col. 3: 5 ff. or the Letter of James.

(e) The use of the Old Testament

We have already seen how Christian worship was shaped, in part, by Jewish forms of worship; we have also noticed that the 'fulfilment' of Jewish scripture was one of the themes of the early apostolic proclamation, or *kerygma*, and of the more elaborate *kerygma* in the Gospels— especially Matthew's (see p. 76). We must now pause to notice how much in the letters of the New Testament, as in these other writings, is concerned with 'the fulfilment of scripture'.

This note of fulfilment seems to be specially charac- teristic of Christianity. Already, before the coming of Jesus, Jewish teachers were busy reinterpreting their ancient sacred books so as to apply them to their own cir- cumstances and needs. From the first five books especially

(Genesis, Exodus, Leviticus, Numbers, Deuteronomy) they could draw a great deal of moral teaching. The Jews call these five books 'the Torah'. This word is often translated 'Law', but that is really too narrow a term. Torah means something more like 'instruction': it is the statement of God's will and ways. In Greek these books were sometimes simply called the Pentateuch, or Five Books. But the Jews read their scriptures not only for moral standards and ethical exhortation, but also as an account of how God had called and shaped a People for himself, and as a forecast of the way in which that People's destiny would be worked out in the future. The Jewish scriptures were thus seen to be forward-looking as well as backward-looking, and they were read with eager expectation by devout Jews who searched for signs that God was still at work in the events of their own day, so as to vindicate his People and bring them to their destiny. Indeed, in the story of the exodus—the emigration—of the oppressed Hebrews from slavery in Egypt, told in the Old Testament book called Exodus, the Jews already had something comparable to the Christians' *kerygma* or proclamation—something that spoke words of hope for the present situation. Deut. 26: 5–9 is a well-known example:

And thou shalt answer and say before the LORD thy God, A Syrian ready to perish was my father, and he went down into Egypt, and sojourned there, few in number; and he became there a nation, great, mighty, and populous: and the Egyptians evil entreated us, and afflicted us, and laid upon us hard bondage: and we cried unto the LORD, the God of our fathers, and the LORD heard our voice, and saw our affliction, and our toil, and our oppression: and the LORD brought us forth out of Egypt with a mighty

hand, and with an outstretched arm, and with great terrible-
ness, and with signs, and with wonders: and he hath brought
us into this place, and hath given us this land, a land flowing with milk and honey.

There is a longer proclamation of this kind in Joshua 24.

The statement at the heart of the Jewish proclamation
was that God had brought his People out of bondage and
entered into a covenant with them through Moses at
Mount Sinai. By this covenant or agreement God bound
his People to himself and himself to his People. He
offered them his protection just as a great king would offer
protection to a subject people; and, like such a king, he
demanded loyalty from them. This rescue from Egypt
and covenant-making at Mount Sinai was the pattern of
God's dealings with them—the standard by which they
might judge subsequent events. Later on, Israel had been
deported to Babylon, but, again, God had brought them
triumphantly back to Palestine and renewed his covenant
with them. And so their hopes for the future followed a
similar pattern. In Daniel 9: 2, the earlier book of
Jeremiah is used in a calculation relating to the present;
and the Dead Sea scrolls, which began to come to light in
1947 (see p. 32), include documents which show how the
prophetic books of the Old Testament were, just before
the Christian era, again being reinterpreted so as to apply
to current events and give hope that God's hand was still
at work to rescue his own People. These can conveniently
be read in the edition by G. Vermès, *The Dead Sea Scrolls
in English* (Penguin Books, 1962).

Thus the pre-Christian Jews had already applied the
scriptures to current events. What these Jewish teachers
of scripture do not seem to have found was anything that
could be truly called fulfilment. The discovery of fulfil-

ment is distinctive of the Christian understanding. Jesus's own message is given in Mark 1: 15 as 'The time has come; the kingdom of God is upon you...'. It is characteristic of the New Testament interpretation of scripture to find in Jesus Christ, and in the sequel to his death and resurrection, the climax, the fulfilment, of Jewish expectation. '...This is what the prophet spoke of...' says Peter in Acts 2: 16; the people of Jerusalem, declares Paul in Acts 13: 27, by condemning Jesus to death had unconsciously fulfilled the very words of the prophets which they had constantly heard read, though without understanding them; 'the proclamation of Jesus Christ'—as the ascription of praise, the 'doxology', at the end of the letter to the Romans puts it—had been 'according to the revelation of that divine secret kept in silence for long ages but now disclosed...' (Rom. 16: 25f.).

Although at first the ministry of Jesus had seemed so unlike the triumph and victory of God's kingdom—for it had been so self-effacing and gentle and had ended in apparent defeat and death—Christians had come to realize that this was, in fact, the fulfilment of God's age-long design. All kinds of different symbols and figures of God's triumph were now found converging on the single figure of Jesus of Nazareth. He was Messiah or Christ (both words mean the divinely appointed king); he was the Son of Man (that is the defenceless human figure who lets obedience to God take him through death to glory); he was the Son of God (the one who trustfully and joyfully does God's will); he was the Suffering Servant (the one whose self-sacrifice in God's cause is found to bring life and relief to others). The agreement or covenant between God and his People, made at Mount Sinai through Moses, had been broken. God had stood by his People, but they had deserted him. Now, the new covenant which Jeremiah foresaw had been fulfilled in Jesus. Once again God and man were bound together by a new agreement, not this time written on stone and ratified by the sacrifice of animals, but inaugurated by God's own Son and ratified by his own voluntary self-sacrifice on the cross. As we have seen, that is precisely why the Christian writings eventually came to be called the New Testament.

Thus, the Jewish scriptures, reinterpreted and brilliantly lit by the new light brought by Jesus, formed an important element in Christian speaking and writing—not least in what is technically called Christian 'apologetic', that is defence or explanation before unbelievers and inquirers.

CHRISTIAN WRITINGS WERE
SHAPED BY CIRCUMSTANCES

Thus, all these elements that we have found reflected in the letters and other writings of the New Testament helped to form the language and expressions of the Christian communities, and so, ultimately, of their writings: *kerygma*, or evangelistic proclamation of the facts; *didache*, or teaching for the evangelized; worship; sermons; and all with reference to the scriptures of the Old Testament. One could, no doubt, analyse out other ingredients, but these were among the chief ones; and we have to try to imagine Christians using them according to their needs in all sorts of different circumstances. The necessity for formulating, and, sooner or later, writing down, their convictions and aspirations and hopes was forced upon them by the situations in which they found themselves—making new converts, teaching them and building them up, fighting error and misunderstandings, solving moral problems, explaining and defending their faith before the hostile or incredulous, or bearing witness to it before their persecutors. The Christian writings were shaped and hammered out in the hard 'blacksmith's shop' of real life—even real death. But the material turned out to be the tempered steel of God's own gift—Christ Jesus, crucified and raised from death.

THE BOOK CALLED THE REVELATION

An extreme instance of a writing hammered out by the pressure of events and in the furnace of distress is the Revelation. It begins with a powerful vision of the risen Christ, and with messages of warning and encouragement to the Christians in seven towns of western Asia Minor. And then follows what is technically known as an *apocalypse*, which is Greek for revelation or unveiling: that is, it is a description in visionary, symbolic, picture-language of the great battle between God and the world-forces of evil—a battle which is, for those who have eyes to see behind the veil, already won. Satan is conquered and cast down; and Christians who are suffering for their faith have only to hold on and not give in, and they will find that they are on the winning side. Indeed, the heart of God's strange victory is 'a Lamb with the marks of slaughter upon him' (Rev. 5: 6): it is precisely by following Jesus to death for God's sake that the People of God will find themselves triumphant.

Years before the Christian era, persecuted Jews had found courage in a visionary 'peep behind the scenes'. There is an extensive Jewish literature of 'apocalypse'—some within the Old Testament, such as parts of Daniel, some in the so-called 'pseudepigraphic' books. These were books written under an assumed name (literally, 'falsely inscribed', from Greek *pseudes*, 'false', and *epigraphein*, 'to inscribe'). They purported to be written by one of the great patriarchs or prophets of long before, but were actually written by later sufferers to convey a message of hope in hard times. Examples are the various books going under the name of Enoch or Baruch. There is a convenient edition of *The Book of Enoch* in translation by R. H. Charles (S.P.C.K. 1917). The Christian book of the Revelation—written not under the false name of some ancient prophet of long before, but openly in the name of a Christian pastor named John—was similarly meant to infuse hope into Christians who were up against it, apparently at a time when it might cost you your life if you refused to offer worship to the Roman Emperor as divine. Unlike the Jewish apocalypses, however, it could actually take its stand upon the fact of Christ, crucified but victorious:

'These men that are robed in white—who are they and from where do they come?' But I answered, 'My lord, you know, not I.' Then he said to me, 'These are the men who have passed through the great ordeal; they have washed their robes and made them white in the blood of the Lamb. That is why they stand before the throne of God and minister to him day and night in his temple; and he who sits on the throne will dwell with them' (Rev. 7: 13-15).

Although the Revelation of John is the only writing of this sort within the New Testament, there are certain passages in other New Testament books which use similar symbols and figures to express the inexpressible and to lift the veil—for apocalypse means lifting the veil—which conceals God's plan from human eyes. Examples

are Mark 13 (parallel to Matthew 24, Luke 21), and
2 Thess. 2: 1–12. Here are some verses taken from these
passages:

But in those days, after that distress, the sun will be darkened,
the moon will not give her light; the stars will come falling
from the sky, the celestial powers will be shaken. Then they
will see the Son of Man coming in the clouds with great
power and glory, and he will send out the angels and gather
his chosen from the four winds, from the farthest bounds of
earth to the farthest bounds of heaven.

Learn a lesson from the fig-tree. When its tender shoots
appear and are breaking into leaf, you know that summer is
near (Mark 13: 24–8).

And then he will be revealed, that wicked man whom the
Lord Jesus will destroy with the breath of his mouth, and
annihilate by the radiance of his coming (2 Thess. 2: 8).

CHRISTIAN WRITINGS NOT INCLUDED IN THE NEW TESTAMENT

We shall soon have to ask: how did the writings which
we now know as the New Testament come to be selected
and grouped together as a collection? But an obviously
prior question is: what else was there to choose from?

That would be an easier question to answer, if it were
possible to name a date at which the selection was made.
But, as we shall see, the New Testament books never
were chosen at a definable moment—as though a selection
committee met and discussed and then announced their
team. The earliest list known to us, coinciding exactly
with the present contents, and offered by a person of
recognized authority in the Church is a letter from the
famous Bishop Athanasius in A.D. 367. But this was really
only making definite something which, in the main, had

already been accepted and recognized over a wide area long before. The settling down of the New Testament canon, or list of recognized books, was a gradual and almost imperceptible process. The word 'canon', by the way, comes from a word shared by both Hebrew and Greek, and seems literally to have meant a reed used as a measuring rod or as a test of straightness; hence any 'standard' by which correctness or authenticity may be tested. 'Cannon' (the weapon) is from the same root, but presumably depends on thinking of a reed as a hollow tube.

It is impossible, then, to say precisely what other competitors for admission were in existence when the selection was made; for the selection was itself a prolonged and gradual process, and Christian writings must have been coming into circulation and dropping out again all the time. However, it is possible to name certain books, which are not now in the New Testament, and of which the earliest were written, probably, earlier than some of the books now included in the canon and even the latest probably still before the earliest authoritative lists, such as Athanasius's. And some of these books, as we shall see, had been, from time to time, used by Christians just as the Bible is used now, for reading aloud and for private study. Here are some of these early Christian writings now outside the New Testament.

(a) The Apostolic Fathers

'Fathers' is a term which used to be applied generally to all Christian writers between the New Testament and, perhaps, the beginning of the Middle Ages. The equivalent Latin term, *patristic* writers, is now more usual. But the name 'the Apostolic Fathers' has been retained to describe the authors of certain Christian documents which seem mainly to belong to the generations immediately following that of the original apostles themselves—some of the earliest Christian literature outside our present New Testament. The writings are the following and may be read in the translation by K. Lake (Loeb Library, 2 vols., 1917–19); the dates added in brackets are only conjectural: The First Letter of Clement, bishop of Rome (A.D. 95); the so-called Second Letter of Clement, though this is certainly not by the same writer (date undetermined); seven Letters of Ignatius, bishop of Antioch (A.D. 117); the Letter of Polycarp, bishop of Smyrna, to the Philippians (?A.D. 135); the account of the Martyrdom of Polycarp (A.D. 155); the Teaching (or *Didache*) of the Apostles (very uncertain: ?A.D. 60 or it may be much later); the Letter of Barnabas (?A.D. 150); the 'Shepherd' of Hermas (?A.D. 140); the Letter to Diognētus (date undetermined).

Clement's letter is addressed to the Christian congregation at Corinth, after the death of Paul, whose own letters to the Corinthians we have. Like Paul's, it expresses concern about disorders in that unruly church. It is a long letter, containing immensely valuable evidence for the thought and organization and manner of worship of Christians in Rome and Corinth soon after the time of Paul. '2 Clement'—the so-called second letter—is really a Christian sermon of unknown authorship and very likely later date.

Ignatius, bishop of Antioch in Syria, condemned to be put to death at Rome as a Christian, though we do not know on precisely what charge, wrote seven letters to Christians in various towns in Asia Minor and in Rome, while he was under arrest and on his long journey to his death. They are an extraordinary manifesto by a man of intense Christian conviction gifted with a startlingly vivid and daringly pictorial way of writing. He is standing up against false teaching about a Christ who never truly became man or was crucified or was raised again, and against disorder and anarchy in the Church. Some of the writing is extravagant—almost fanatical; but there is an impressive grasp of essentials. It is the last 'testament' of a man triumphantly on his way to lay down his life in witness. One of the letters of Ignatius, the only one to an individual, is to Bishop Polycarp of Smyrna, who was himself eventually martyred; and we have a letter from Polycarp to the Christians at Philippi, and a more or less contemporary, though in parts legendary, account of his brave death.

The so-called *Didache* or Teaching of the Twelve Apostles is a curious little 'manual' of Christian practice. It is in some respects strangely primitive and doctrinally undeveloped; but it is still debated whether this indicates an early date or whether it is from a later but still un-developed community or even whether it is a deliberate effort by a later writer to portray the outlook of an earlier age. There is a brief quotation from this writing on p. 94.

The so-called Letter of Barnabas is almost certainly not by the Barnabas mentioned in the Acts (4: 36, etc.). It is an extreme example of one of the ways in which Christians treated the Jewish scriptures. Within the New Testament the Jewish scriptures are sometimes taken as an account of God's dealings with his People, to which Christians saw Christ as the climax and coping-stone; sometimes as a kind of foreshadowing of, or preparation for, the coming of Christ. But 'Barnabas', adopting an extreme position, interprets the Jewish scriptures as a kind of message from God in code. They were never intended, he argues, to be taken literally: the Jews were mistaken in actually offering animal sacrifices, and observing food-taboos, and practising circumcision, and so forth. All this, if one has the decoding rules, can be read, he maintains, as simply predictions about the coming of Christ and the Christian way of life. To treat scripture as 'Barnabas' does is merely to force upon it what is really derived from elsewhere and already believed on other independent grounds. The Letter of Barnabas served as a stick with which to beat those non-Christian Jews who used the same methods in interpreting scripture for their own purposes; but it did not give any new authority to what was being affirmed. The method adopted by 'Barnabas' is a way of bending Jewish scripture to Christian belief, a way which cannot commend itself to an honest mind. It implies a view of God's ways of revealing himself which is alien to all that the life of Christ seems to teach us.

The 'Shepherd' of Hermas is a long and extraordinary book. Its title comes from the fact that the angel who, in a certain section of the book, is reported as teaching Hermas, comes before him in the form of a shepherd. This Hermas was a Christian living at Rome; and he adopted a method rather like that which Bunyan was to use some 1600 years later when he wrote *The Pilgrim's Progress*. 'The Shepherd' is a kind of allegory: in picture-language, the writer conveys his convictions about various matters of Christian life and discipline. He is specially concerned with the problem caused by sin after baptism, and with the possibility of repentance and restoration.

Finally, the anonymous 'Letter to Diognētus' is a gracious and attractive little defence of the Christian way of life. But, for all its charm, it is content to stay on a level, typical of much of the non-Jewish Christianity of the Greek world, where Christ is viewed more as an example than a divine bringer of power, and Christianity more as just a way of life than as faith and worship. It is instructive to read 'Diognētus' side by side with the description of early Christian proclamation in the Acts (see pp. 69 f.).

(b) Other Gospels and Acts, etc.

Of the Apostolic Fathers—the writings which have just been reviewed—only the letters are comparable in form to any writings of the New Testament. But there are other books which, in one way or another, are concerned with the story of Jesus and his disciples, and are, in this respect, comparable to the Gospels and the Acts. But, whereas the Apostolic Fathers survive practically complete, these other writings survive only incompletely or, in some cases, are known of only because they are mentioned in early writers.

For instance, there are the following: the Book of James (much later—in the sixteenth century—called the *Protevangelium*, or preliminaries to the Gospel, of James); the Syriac Gospel of Thomas; the History of Joseph the Carpenter; the Transition (i.e. journey to Heaven) of the Blessed Virgin; the Gospel of Peter. The collective description given to writings like these is 'apocryphal writings'. *Apocrypha* is the Greek for 'hidden things'; but it has come to mean writings not included in an official canon or list. The reason why these were not included in the New Testament list is generally obvious. Most of them are feeble in ideas and wildly fanciful and fantastic, and practically worthless either as history or literature; and very often they can be seen to have been written in order to convey heretical ideas (ideas rejected by the Church) of the nature of Jesus Christ. Most of them are late, from the late second to the fifth and sixth centuries, and, so far as they are based on historical sources at all, simply draw freely and inaccurately on the four Gospels.

Then, apart from full 'Gospels', there were collections of the sayings of Jesus. Some such collections, now no longer surviving independently, no doubt lie behind the four Gospels. But there are only a few collections independently known: for instance, the Greek ones on papyrus found at a place in Egypt called Oxyrhynchus; and some in Coptic, one of the languages of Egypt, on sheets of papyrus found at another Egyptian site, Cheno-boskion or Nag Hammādi. The best known of these is called the Gospel of Thomas, conveniently available in the Fontana edition (1960) as *The Secret Sayings of Jesus*, by R. M. Grant and D. L. Freedman, but it is to be distinguished, as a mere collection of sayings, from the Syriac Gospel of Thomas just referred to. Some of the sayings in these two documents are clearly parallel to each other; and some in the Thomas collection are like some in the New Testament, including whole parables. It seems that the Thomas sayings belong to a gnostic sect. The term gnostic (see p. 84) is used to describe people who, though often claiming to be Christians, did not believe in a real, historical 'incarnation', that is they did not believe that God himself really 'became flesh', and they followed secret, mystic speculations of their own. They mostly believed that matter—the whole material world—was by nature evil, and that the good God could not have created it; and since they made a sharp distinction between spirit and matter, it followed that they could not believe that God had come into this world as man, for to them to become flesh meant to partake of evil.

Then there were 'Acts'—that is, stories of Christian figures, or of others connected with the Christian story, for instance, the Acts of John—imaginary tales of this apostle's travels—the Acts of Paul, including a section known as the Acts of Paul and Thecla, the Acts of Peter, the Acts of Andrew, the Acts of Thomas. Also—to complete the apocryphal counterparts of different types of New Testament writings—there are various letters and apocalypses or revelations said to be by New Testament figures.

Nothing brings home more vividly the dignity and restraint and truthfulness of the writings of the New Testament than to compare them with these attempts to improve on them—attempts which are, most or all, later and heretical and feeble and fanciful in the extreme. You can conveniently read English translations of some of them in M. R. James, *The Apocryphal New Testament* (1924), or in *New Testament Apocrypha*, translated by R. McL. Wilson (from a German book by E. Hennecke, edited by W. Schneemelcher) (1963). There is a first-rate brief description of them in F. L. Cross, *The Early Christian Fathers* (1960), ch. v. A very useful exercise is to compare the character of Jesus as it strikes a reader of Mark with the character seen in, say, the Syriac Gospel of Thomas, where the child Jesus is a miniature magician with no moral qualities whatever and no reality about him.

THE CANON OF THE NEW TESTAMENT

This short sketch of the Apostolic Fathers and apocryphal New Testament has brought us back to the difficult and important question: what led to the writings which we now know as the New Testament being collected together and set apart from the rest—and who did it?

(a) The oral period

As we have already seen (pp. 64 f.), the first Christians started with no writings of their own. When distinctively Christian writings did begin to take shape, they sprang quite naturally—almost incidentally—out of the needs of the Christian communities, and their writers probably had no idea that they would eventually be collected together into a book like the Jewish scriptures and be placed alongside, and indeed above, the Jewish scriptures. The only *written* authority they started with was the *Jewish* 'Bible'—the scriptures which Christians now call the Old Testament. When the writer of 2 Tim. 4: 13 asked for his notebooks (see p. 64), he had no inkling that these, or writings like them, would themselves perhaps one day become 'scripture'. 'Scripture', of course, only means something in writing; but it has come to mean *authoritative* writing—something which a given body of people recognize as carrying some kind of authority—divine authority, it may be.

Thus, during the earliest years of the Christian Church's existence, the Church's authority lay primarily in the spoken evidence of eyewitnesses and in the witness of its Christian life. The twelve apostles had been specially chosen by Jesus himself to be with him and commissioned to go and give evidence about him. And, although one of them, Judas, turned traitor and betrayed him, Acts 1: 15 ff. tells how the gap was filled by the special election of Matthias in his place. In addition, therefore, to countless others who, as witnesses of the events, were able to give evidence, here was a body of twelve men whose special commission it was to 'authenticate' the facts—to give authoritative evidence of Jesus and his resurrection. The

number twelve was no doubt meant as a deliberate reminder that the Christian Church saw itself as the real
heart of the twelve tribes of Israel, that is, God's People
who, right through the Old Testament scriptures, are seen
as chosen to bear witness to God.

Naturally, therefore, and almost without their realizing
what was happening, the witness of these persons mingled
with the witness of the Jewish scriptures. A new and
overwhelming authority—the authority of the risen
Christ in and through his witnesses—had sprung up alongside the Jewish scriptures and came eventually to dominate
them, as the climax dominates a story, or as the coping-
stone dominates the entire archway. The idea of Christ as
fulfiller of the Old Testament carries within it the idea
of the authority of Jewish scripture leading into and
becoming secondary to that of Christian witness. It is this
that gives unity to the Bible as a whole, and makes it
necessary for Christians to use the Old Testament as well
as the New.

(b) Written records

But, as time passed, the first generation, the eyewitness
generation, grew old and began to die. It was obviously
important that their witness should be made more
permanent by being committed to writing. And so there
arose bits and pieces of Christian record—often, one may
guess, written not by the twelve apostles themselves—for
their primary task was witness by life and work and word
—but by their disciples and assistants and followers. Thus
it is that the early historian Eusebius, bishop of Caesarea,
writing in Greek in about A.D. 320, tells us, as we have
seen (pp. 73 f.), that Papias, bishop of Hierapolis in about
A.D. 130, recorded a tradition that Mark had written

down what he had heard Peter say when, from time to time, he preached and taught. This is part, at least, of the material that seems to have gone eventually into what we now know as Mark's Gospel. In the same way, traditional teaching by Matthew and John seems to have found its way into the Gospels now known by their names. Luke is not known even to have been a close follower of any of the twelve; but he was a careful collector of traditions, both written and spoken, and made his Gospel out of these.

Meanwhile, apart from these documents which preserved sayings of Jesus and stories of his life, there were beginning to be, as we have seen, letters of teaching and advice from such outstanding leaders as Paul.

(c) Collecting begins

In each of the churches founded by Paul there would probably be treasured the one or two letters he had addressed to that particular community. Clement of Rome, addressing the Corinthian Christians, tells them, in 1 Clement 47: 1, the letter mentioned on p. 106, to 'Take up the letter of the blessed Paul the Apostle', implying that they had at least one safely stored away. But in many cases Christians possessing a letter from Paul probably did not know that any others existed elsewhere. The reference in Col. 4: 16 to an exchange of letters between the towns of Colossae and Laodicea may be an exception; and in any case Colossae and Laodicea were near neighbours. It must have been at a later stage that the idea of making a collection of Paul's letters caught on. Whether it was the idea of one individual, or whether bit by bit a collection of one or two grew, like a snowball, into something bigger, we cannot say for certain. But by the time of the interesting heretic Marcion (about

A.D. 140), we meet a collection of Paul's letters, including all that are now recognized as his.

Thus, bit by bit, the Church which had begun with no literature except the Jewish scriptures found itself possessed of writings of its own. But we have to remember that there was no such thing as printing in those days, or even duplicating; and therefore there was nothing quite like what we know as 'publishing' a book. It was a comparatively rare thing for any writing to be copied or reproduced in any quantity. And therefore the different Christian writings must at first have been only locally known, and confined to their respective centres.

(d) The Four Gospel canon

For a time, Mark's may have been the only Gospel known to Christians in Rome—for that is where it is generally placed—and conversely, the Roman Christians may have been the only people who knew of it. Mark, which is almost certainly the earliest of our Gospels, was quite probably written later than Paul's letters; and Matthew, Luke and John later still. One might have expected that eventually either the Church would have chosen one of the four and dispensed with the rest; or a single composite Gospel would have been made out of them all; or else many more than four would have been accepted.

As a matter of fact, there were times when any of these things might have happened. A certain Tatian did actually make a 'harmony' of the four—a single, combined Gospel woven together from bits of them all. It was called Tatian's *Diatessaron* (the Greek for 'through four' or 'by means of four'—it was Tatian's creation of one out of all four), and we possess fragments of it; but it never finally established itself. Again, there was a time when Matthew's Gospel seemed so satisfactory—including, as it did, practically all Mark's material and much besides, and beautifully arranged—that it seemed likely to oust Mark and become the sole Gospel. And that same heretic Marcion made exclusive use of an edition of Luke modified by him according to his own beliefs. Furthermore, there were, as we saw on p. 109, certain other writings claiming to be Gospels that might have been added to the four. For instance, there is a very curious incident recorded by the Greek historian of the Church, Eusebius, whom we have already met. He says that a certain Serapion, bishop of Antioch in about A.D. 200, had given his approval to the use of that same Gospel of Peter, mentioned on p. 109, by the Christians in a town called Rhossus in Cilicia, in Asia Minor; but that Bishop Serapion later found out that there were heretical additions in it—all who have read the recovered fragments of the Gospel of Peter could have told him that!—and he therefore withdrew his approval.

Thus, there were actually signs, at one time or another, of a single composite Gospel being made out of the four, or of one of the four dominating the scene, or of the number being indefinitely increased. Why, despite all this, did the four, Matthew, Mark, Luke, and John, stand their ground, and stand alone? The answer seems to be made up of several factors. In the first place, all four seem to have genuinely apostolic connexions and to be based on early and authentic material; and so far no trace has appeared of any other complete Gospel with anything like such strong claims to genuineness. Then, again, it is by no means certain that any rival Gospel existed until a later date. All the other Gospels about which we know anything seem to be later, with the possible exception of a no longer surviving Hebrew or Aramaic one. It is true that Luke 1: 1 mentions 'many writers' who, before him, had 'undertaken to draw up an account of the events...'; but perhaps, apart from Mark, he had in mind not any complete Gospel, but merely collections of sayings and anecdotes which may well have been in circulation. Thus, it may well be that Matthew, Mark, Luke, and John were positively the only Gospels with early and authentic roots. Finally, each of these four was probably connected with one well established Christian community, and belonged to it; and it is easy to understand that the centre from which Mark, for example, originated would be unwilling to give up its own Gospel in favour of Matthew, while Matthew's centre would be unwilling to exchange it for Mark, even by the time both these Gospels were circulating freely among all the Christian centres. This being so, the only answer was for all to recognize and use them all.

Thus, by A.D. 180 Irenaeus, bishop of Lyons, affirms that it is as natural and as necessary that there should be four Gospels as that there should be four points of the compass, and so forth!

(e) Tests for inclusion in the canon

Luke's Gospel brought with it 'volume two', the Acts of the Apostles; and, besides the great and recognized letters of Paul, there came the two to Timothy and one to Titus (now often called the Pastoral Epistles), the Letter to the Hebrews, and several letters claiming various apostolic names. Once again, we know (see pp. 106 ff.) of other letters; but none of these is as early as Paul's, and few even of the later letters now within the New Testament are as late as most of these others; besides, most of these rival letters—1 Clement, Barnabas, the Letter to

Diognētus, even Ignatius's very striking letters—are inferior in their grasp of the heart of the Christian gospel and are less clearly connected with the circle of the apostles than practically all the New Testament letters.

Thus, broadly speaking, it is early date, apostolic contacts, and intrinsic soundness that seem to have brought in the letters that did come in. But the process was not a smooth one. There are two or three passages in early writings which provide evidence of a certain fluctuation and uncertainty. It is important to remember, however, that, even here, the central nucleus of writings was not in question: the doubt attached only to a few, mostly on the circumference. Here are specimens of early writings reflecting the debates over genuineness (see J. Stevenson, *A New Eusebius* (S.P.C.K. 1957), pp. 146, 337f.):

The Epistle of Jude no doubt, and the couple bearing the name of John, are accepted in the Catholic Church; and the Wisdom written by the friends of Solomon in his honour. The Apocalypse also of John, and of Peter only we receive, which some of our friends will not have read in the Church. But the Shepherd was written quite lately in our times in the city of Rome by Hermas, while his brother Pius, the bishop, was sitting in the chair of the church of the city of Rome; and therefore it ought indeed to be read, but it cannot to the end of time be publicly read in the Church to the people, either among the prophets, who are complete in number, or among the Apostles.

But of Arsinous, called also Valentinus, or of Miltiades we receive nothing at all; those who have also composed a new book of Psalms for Marcion, together with Basileides and the Asian founder of the Cataphrygians are rejected (From the fragmentary list of about A.D. 190, published in 1740 by Muratori and called the Muratorian Canon).

Of Peter, then, one epistle, his former as it is called, is

acknowledged; and of this also the elders of olden time have made frequent use, as a work beyond dispute, in their own treatises. But as for the second extant [epistle,] the tradition received by us is that it is not canonical; nevertheless, since it appeared profitable to many, store was set by it along with the other Scriptures. Yet as regards the book of his Acts, as it is entitled, and the Gospel named after him, and his Preaching, as it is called, and The Apocalypse (such is its name): we know that they were not handed down at all among the catholic [writings]; for no Church writer, either in ancient times or even in our day, used testimonies derived from them.

But as my history advances I shall deem it profitable to indicate, along with the successions, what Church writers in each period have made use of which of the disputed [books], and what they have said about the canonical and acknowledged writings, and anything that they have said about those that are not such.

Now the writings that bear the name of Peter, of which I recognize only one epistle as genuine and acknowledged by the elders of olden time, are so many; while the fourteen epistles of Paul are manifest and clear [as regards their genuineness]. Nevertheless it is not right to be ignorant that some have rejected the Epistle to the Hebrews, saying that it is disputed by the church of the Romans as not being Paul's. And I shall quote at the proper time what those who lived before us have said with reference to this epistle also. Moreover, I have not received his Acts, as they are called, among the undisputed writings (Eusebius, *Ecclesiastical History*, III. 3. 1–5, written in Greek, about A.D. 320).

When we look at the story as a whole, the collection of early Christian writings looks rather like what a living cell looks like under a microscope—a fairly well defined nucleus or centre, namely, the solid core of writings that early established themselves decisively and were virtually never challenged, and round it a more nebulous and filmy area where there is more uncertainty, namely, the area in which 2 Peter and 2 and 3 John flow in and out, in company with Barnabas and Hermas, 1 Clement and the rest.

Little by little the 'cell' becomes better defined. Besides, there were heretics and there was persecution. In a Church where there was no heresy and no disputing and no oppression from outside, there would be no need even to draw up a definitive list. But in fact the Church did have to face just such troubles as these. The people who claimed to be Christians but who held ideas which the Christian world as a whole recognized as out of tune with the dominant notes of the tradition had to be met and replied to; and how could that be done successfully if the Church as a whole had no definition of its own authoritative writings? It was precisely because of the heretical contents of the writings to which these men appealed—like those additions to the Gospel of Peter condemned by Bishop Serapion (see p. 116)—that the Church had to reach a decision about which to exclude and which to recognize. And again, in times of persecution it mattered which books were sacred and not to be surrendered, and which did not signify. Long before this, as we have seen, the bulk of the Christian writings had, by prolonged usage, asserted themselves. But now, for the sake of defending the truth, they had to be officially and formally defined. And that is what led to the official lists such as Bishop Athanasius's in his letter of A.D. 367.

Even when a list is drawn up, it does not necessarily imply that everything outside the list is inferior—still less bad. It is only as much as to say 'the Church recognizes and accepts these books as the authentic reflexion of the decisive events which brought the Church into existence: about other writings we are not ready to make assertions'.

4

HOW THE NEW TESTAMENT
CAME TO US

We have just read how the books of our present New Testament came to be written, and how after a time they came to be selected and regarded as the official writings of Christianity. This took about 350 years. During all this time, both the writings we now have in the New Testament and the other writings which were not eventually included were circulating among Christian people. They were written in the first place for the instruction and encouragement of these people, and they continued to be used for this. Men read them, thought about them, explained them to other Christians, and quoted them in argument with non-Christians. Whenever anyone wanted a copy of any part of what was later to become the New Testament, it would have to be made by hand and was always a fragile object, liable to be damaged or destroyed.

CHANGES OF WORDING

When we want to study the New Testament today we need to know how the contents have been handed down to us. We also need to know whether we have any documents which were actually written in the earliest days, or any which can be shown to have been carefully copied from those documents, and whether there have been changes, great or small, by mistake or by intention. When we look into this, we find that we possess a great deal of material, but that there are noticeable differences between different manuscripts. Evidently at an early period, great changes took place. When we look at the variations of wording, we find that there are groups of manuscripts which share the same wording in certain places. We study next how these groups are related, and how the changes took place and why: and also which manuscripts have been copied from which others. In this way, we can find our way through the mass of variations towards the original.

Anyone can make a simple experiment to help himself understand how some changes took place. Take any book and copy out a long passage. Better still, have someone dictate it to you. Then compare what you have written with what is printed in the book. You will find that a mistake or so has already crept in—words are missed out or repeated, a whole line may be jumped, a word is misspelt or a familiar word substituted for a less familiar word which sounds or looks like it. Imagine that this copying process is repeated many times. It is clear that there will be in the end many differences. Some of them may be important. No one is infallible in this: so that some mistakes of this kind could creep in, quite accidentally, early in the course of copying. It is this process which we mean when we talk about the 'corruption' of a text. For instance, in all manuscripts of 1 Cor. 6: 5 the Greek means 'to judge between his brother', which makes no sense: very early the words 'a brother and' were left out after 'between', and we need to supply them, as indeed an early translation has done. The New English Bible ignores the difficulty and translates 'to give a decision in a brother-Christian's cause'. Sometimes words which sound the same but are spelt differently can be found, like 'way' and 'weigh' in English. At times the one which seemed to fit the sense better has taken the place of a harder word which originally stood there. The word *kamelos* a camel, and *kamilos* a ship's hawser, sounded the same in Greek at this time: in the saying about a camel going through a needle's eye (Matt. 19: 24; Mark 10: 25; Luke 18: 25) some scribes and some commentators have quite missed the point of utter impossibility which Jesus intended when he talked about a camel and have written the word for a hawser, which is not such a striking paradox.

This brings us to another type of change in the transmission of these books: deliberate change. When men were reading and explaining the scriptures, attention would concentrate on the difficult places. These might be changed, so that the text now gave, or as we say 'read', something more readily understood, or words might be added as an explanation of the difficulty or to smooth it away. So in Mark 1: 41 a word translated as 'moved with pity' (N.E.B. 'Jesus was sorry for him') has been substituted in most manuscripts for a word translated 'moved with anger' (N.E.B. 'In warm indignation'). Again in John 7: 39 many manuscripts read 'there was no spirit yet' which in others has been expanded to read 'there was no spirit yet given' (as the N.E.B. reads, 'the Spirit had not yet been given'). The reason for these alterations is evident, and they give rise to two rules which can be applied to the solution of differences in wording between the manuscripts. The first rule is 'the shorter reading is to be accepted', and the second is 'the harder reading is to be accepted'. These rules sometimes have exceptions: for instance, one ancient manuscript of the book of Revelation shows a tendency to remove some of the difficulties by shortening the text. In this case one would not accept the shorter readings. But as a starting point these rules are of value.

The New Testament was originally written in Greek, the language of many communities in the Eastern Mediterranean. Greek has a long history and a wonderful literature, and it was moulded into a means of expressing subtle thought by philosophers. After the conquests of Alexander the Great it became the language of many people who were not Greek by birth, and who in the earliest generations did not speak Greek as a native language but as a language for trade and government, much as English is used in many countries outside England and the U.S.A. The Greek which they spoke was not always the pure Greek to be found in the great poetry and prose of Greece. Fine shades of meaning and careful turns of phrase tended to disappear, although Greek still remained a beautiful language even in this period and capable of expressing thought and argument. Some of the New Testament is written by men who evidently had some education, but much of it by ordinary folk without much book-learning. So their Greek is rough and at times reflects the non-Greek language in which they still thought (the Aramaic language in the case of the New Testament). This too led to alterations later. For when the Church began to attract more men of education into its ranks, and after the Roman persecutions were over, there was time to think about the sacred books as works of literature as well as works of faith. Then educated men came to find some of the ways of speech rather ugly or awkward, and to think that this kind of language was not fitting for the scriptures. So some changes came about by men's attempts to improve the grammar or the style, to cut out words which they considered dialect or slang, and to make the whole flow more smoothly.

We can trace all these processes of change and altera-

tion, intentional and unintentional, because there are still
preserved many manuscripts of the Greek New Testament
in which these variations can be seen. Although changes
took place they did not take place all at once, nor did
changes meet with everyone's approval or come into
fashion everywhere. There were in different places and in
different centuries, different fashions of 'polished' and
'edited' texts which we call 'recensions'. In other places
(often, those most distant from the centres of civilization)
older texts persisted which had not been so polished or
edited ('text' means the form of words found in a
particular manuscript or group of manuscripts or translation). Even towards the end of the Middle Ages, when
some uniformity had been attained, we still find texts of
all types known and copied. The student of this aspect
of the New Testament must be acquainted with manuscripts of all ages. The earlier a manuscript is, the more
important it may be for his study, but valuable material
constantly turns up in many a late source.

ANCIENT MANUSCRIPTS

Manuscripts are a fascinating study in themselves. To
quote a racy characterization by the New Testament
scholar Robert Casey, a manuscript is 'something between
a gadget and a personality'. That is to say, it is not only a
product of technical skill; it bears the stamp upon it of
the men who created the text and used the manuscript in
their life and worship.

The production of books in antiquity and in the Middle
Ages, their binding, the way the pages were set out, the
ways of their copying and correction—all these things
can affect our understanding of the transmission of the

New Testament. Especially important is the study of styles and methods of writing, a study known as palaeography. It is possible to date the manuscripts of certain periods by the style of writing used in them. This can be done by comparing them with dated documents, usually legal documents or letters. Documents written in the same style may be placed within the same period, and sometimes even shown to come from the same place. In the earliest period we can distinguish a script used for works of literature from a faster-written flowing script with the letters joined together found in letters, notebooks and such-like. The earlier biblical manuscripts are usually written in this slower more formal kind of writing with separated letters rather like capitals, which is called 'uncial' (literally 'inch-high') or 'majuscule'. By about the ninth century a new formal style was invented on the basis of the more flowing style of classical times. This is a very beautiful script and is called 'cursive' (flowing) or 'minuscule'. When it came into vogue, probably through the influence of centres of copying in monasteries of Constantinople, it was widely used for biblical manuscripts. Hence, among manuscripts of the New Testament, an uncial is usually older than a minuscule: but this does not necessarily make it more important to the student of textual change.

Manuscripts could be made of papyrus, parchment or paper. Papyrus was made from reeds, split down the middle, laid side by side. Two layers, one vertical, one horizontal, were then glued together and pressed firm. It was a good and durable material. It was used throughout the then civilized world, but most of what is still preserved has come from Egypt where the hot climate and the dry sand have permitted its survival. The earliest papyri are scrolls, made up of pieces stuck edge to edge, written upon only on one side and then rolled on rollers. Later, books such as we use today were made. These used papyrus, not in long rolls but in separate pages held together in a binding. Instead of unrolling the long scroll, one turned the pages, which were written on both sides. A book of this kind is called a 'codex' (plural 'codices'). Very few manuscripts of the New Testament are scrolls: most are codices. In many cases we have only fragments of papyrus, but in recent years we have been fortunate to discover, especially in Egypt, New Testament books on papyrus in a very good state of preservation. Such are the Chester Beatty New Testament manuscripts, now in Dublin, and the Bodmer papyri in Geneva.

Papyri containing quite different material can be of great importance to the New Testament scholar. Many are letters, business documents, legal documents, school exercises. From them we have learnt much which literature could not teach us about the way in which unlearned people spoke and wrote in the times when the gospel was just spreading and the New Testament coming into being. As we have mentioned, the books of the New Testament were written by such people in their own way, not by literary men. Much in the New Testament that was once hard to understand has become clear from these other papyri. Before they were found, we already had some ideas about this from inscriptions and from potsherds or 'ostraca' (pieces of broken pottery used like scrap-paper in ancient times). The papyri have given us much more knowledge of the same kind. For instance, in 2 Cor. 1: 22, the Spirit is called 'first instalment' or 'pledge' (N.E.B.) and in the New Testament *parousia* is often used to describe the coming of Jesus. 'Pledge' is a translation of the word *arrabōn*, often met in the papyri as a common business term. *Parousia* is a term of religion describing the appearing of the hidden god and a term of civic affairs referring to the visit of a high official.

Most of our manuscripts are made of parchment, that is, the dried and smoothed skins of animals. Not many New Testament manuscripts made entirely of paper are to be found; paper manuscripts are therefore treated together with parchment in all studies. Manuscripts may be found written in a variety of arrangements. Some, including most papyrus manuscripts, have only one column to the page. Some have several columns, for instance the Codex Sinaiticus, which is in the British Museum, has four. Some are quite plain, some lavishly illustrated by little pictures called illuminations or miniatures. Some are large, for use in public worship or in a library, some small for private use. Some have a few notes or signs to indicate where passages are to be found, some contain a full commentary upon the book written in them. Some contain the whole of the New Testament, others just one book or a group such as Paul's Letters. Some present the text of the complete book, some only the portions prescribed for public reading in services. Examples are often exhibited by the museums and libraries where the manuscripts now are: in England, at the British Museum, the Cambridge University Library, and the John Rylands Library in Manchester. Although parchment generally wears better than papyrus, even parchment manuscripts can be found in a fragmentary state.

A special difficulty is met in palimpsests, that is, manuscripts which have been used more than once. At certain periods when parchment was scarce, it was customary to take an old manuscript which was no longer in use, and with pumice to rub out as far as possible the old writing: hence the name palimpsest which means 'twice rubbed'. The manuscript could then be used again. If the scholar of today is interested in the writing that has been erased, he must try to read what was there originally, through the upper writing. This cannot always be done with the naked eye: so means have been devised, as modern science has developed, to overcome some of the difficulties. A chemical can be applied as a reagent, to bring out the under writing for long enough for it to be deciphered. The manuscript may also be read under ultra-violet rays, which help the faint writing to be seen more clearly. Sometimes binocular microscopes may be used. Modern technical skills have greatly helped the study of manuscripts, not only in these ways but by photographic aids such as microfilms, by which the scholar may read a manuscript without the expense of long journeys, and difficult conditions of study.

ANCIENT TRANSLATIONS

In tracing changes in the wording of the New Testament, the scholar does not only use manuscripts in Greek. Translations were made from the Greek text from early times, and they help us to trace the extent to which different forms of the text were known and how they had spread at different periods. Sometimes we can reconstruct from translations readings which in the original Greek have largely disappeared, either because the earlier manuscripts which presumably contained them have disappeared or been destroyed or because of editorial revisions.

In Italy, Gaul, Spain and the Roman province of North

Africa, Latin was the spoken language, and some parts of the New Testament were already translated into Latin by the end of the second century. From evidence in manuscripts and quotations, it would appear that there were several different attempts at translation, and revisions of these attempts; we even find manuscripts in which combinations of attempts are to be found. There was eventually so much variety that in the fourth century Pope Damasus asked the scholar Jerome to undertake an authorized revision of the whole Latin Bible: this revision we now call the Vulgate (that is, the 'commonly used translation').

On the further side of the Roman empire was a wide area stretching from the Mediterranean to Mesopotamia where Syriac was the spoken language. Several translations of differing age are found in that language. At first a 'Gospel harmony', Tatian's *Diatessaron* (see p. 115), a narrative built up from all four Gospels, was used by the Church. Later there was a version (translation) of the Gospels, Acts and Paul's letters which we call the Old Syriac, of which few manuscripts have survived. Later still there was a revision called the Peshitta or Simple version. This is a version still used throughout the east by churches whose services are still held in Syriac, which is no longer widely spoken. Two later very literal versions are also known, and another in a dialect of Syriac which was spoken in Palestine.

In Egypt, the language was Coptic, divided into several different dialects. Translations and revisions were made in all these from very early days, and we possess many manuscripts. They were made directly from Greek and through them we can learn much about the earliest Greek form of the New Testament.

Other versions were made from these but are not of

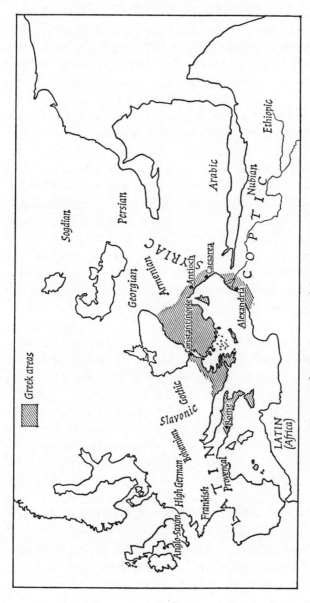

Fig. 5. The expansion of the New Testament.

Greek areas

Anglo-Saxon
Frankish
High German
Bohemian
Provençal
LATIN
Rome
LATIN (Africa)
Slavonic
Gothic
Constantinople
Georgian
Armenian
SYRIAC
Antioch
Caesarea
Alexandria
COPTIC
Nubian
Ethiopic
Arabic
Persian
Sogdian

such importance: however they sometimes contain important traces of the history of the earlier versions. If we trace these versions on a map we shall see that they are languages spoken further away from the centre of the empire, often in independent kingdoms: so we have Armenian, Georgian, Persian and Sogdian from deeper within Asia, Ethiopic, Nubian and Arabic from further south. Other versions were translated from Greek but at too late a period to be of great importance; these were the Gothic, for the Goths settled in the Balkans, and the Old Slavonic, translated in the tenth century when the Slavs were first converted to Christianity. The Goths carried their version with them on their migrations and it had an influence in the west upon some Latin manuscripts.

A further source of information on the text is to be found in the quotations from the New Testament made by ancient Christian writers, both those orthodox in their faith (generally called 'The Fathers', see p. 105) and those later judged to have been in error, or heretical. The date of a manuscript does not always tell us all that can be known about the text which it contains: such a text may have come from far earlier times or once have had a far larger circulation than would appear from the number of manuscripts of this kind which we now have. If the quotations of the text made by some writer agree with the manuscript in a significant number of readings, we can be sure that a text like that of the manuscript was known in the time of that writer and in the place where he lived and worked. Two instances of the results of this method can be briefly mentioned.

There is a form of Latin translation preserved in two manuscripts of the fourth or fifth century, both probably written in the west. But it is known as the African Latin and appears to be the oldest form of translation because it agrees closely with the quotations of Cyprian, who was bishop of Carthage from A.D. 248 until he was martyred in A.D. 258. A more complicated line of research led to the identification of the text of some late minuscules as that which was used sometimes by Origen, a great Christian teacher and martyr, who worked in Alexandria and Caesarea at about the same time as Cyprian lived in Africa. Scholars began first of all by studying these minuscules, because they seemed to present a mixture of readings from two quite distinct and early types. Then an uncial manuscript was discovered, and this proved to have a text closely related to this group; this suggested that the text was earlier than had been suspected. Further comparison showed that Origen used this text in writings composed when he was in Caesarea: hence the text came to be called the 'Caesarean text'. But it was later observed that in fact Origen knew this text while he was still in Alexandria, so that it was not known only in Caesarea but more widely. Two further facts confirmed this: the oldest Georgian version was shown to have this type of text, and a papyrus of the Gospels dated about A.D. 250 was found to be closely related to it.

METHODS OF STUDY

Work with these materials involves so much knowledge and so many skills that textual criticism must be a matter for team-work. Let us draw an ideal sketch of the process. Every manuscript is studied; its origin and descent, and the circumstances of its copying are investigated. It is then compared with some accepted standard: this may be any printed text which scholars agree to use. Thus its variations are known, and can be compared with those of other manuscripts. This can be done for the Greek and also for any translation; for each manuscript of a translation must be studied before we can know what the original wording of the translation was. Within the translation there will probably be a history of change and revision, which must also be known. For any Father, we need first of all a good edition of his whole works so that we may be quite sure of the exact way in which he knew and quoted the New Testament. On the basis of all this preliminary work, we build a critical apparatus, that is, a list of all the variations known, or in other cases a list of those readings which are of evident importance for tracing the history of the text. These variations must then be studied, their origin understood (see p. 122), and the original text of the New Testament built up. We can then find how corruption, revision and change came about, and establish a history of textual change.

This is an ideal picture, for no part of all this process is yet accomplished: we cannot wait for perfection in one task before we move on to the next. We have to work for the time being with the materials we have and continually review our results as new evidence comes to light. Often such a review will tell us which piece of work will next be of importance. At present, many Greek manuscripts remain unknown in detail: some translations, e.g. Latin, are well known, others, e.g. Coptic, not yet known to the full extent of the materials available: not every Father's work has been studied for this purpose. We can establish a text very near to the original, but not certain in every detail; we can trace the history of textual change, but not every period is known with certainty or can be at present.

HANDING DOWN THE TEXT

The main lines of development ran somewhat in this way. In the beginning the writings of the New Testament were not gathered together into one book, and, as we have seen (p. 64), were not in most cases thought of as together forming a 'New Testament'. In the case of the letters of Paul, which we will deal with first, it appears that they lay neglected for some years. Primitive corruptions such as that we have already mentioned in 1 Cor. 6:5 probably go back to this period. Round about A.D. 90, the letters were gathered together and after that time they were handed on as one book.

Our earliest traces of Paul's writings are in the quotations of such early Christian Fathers as Clement of Rome (about A.D. 96) and Ignatius of Antioch (about A.D. 115). Somewhat later the heretical teacher Marcion, from Pontus in Asia Minor, published an edition of Paul, whose thought he believed he understood, but whose words he sometimes altered to confirm his own opinions. Marcion's edition is lost except for the quotations from it by his opponents: what we can recover in this way shows us that readings now known only in the Latin versions were current in Asia in the early second century. Some of Marcion's changes have survived too: these are usually quite obviously changes and do not mislead us.

From the third century we have actual manuscripts of Paul's letters. These show us that the mistakes and changes which we can discern in the second century are indeed present in the text, but that they are not so many as we might have feared. The correct and original reading is usually to be found in some group of manuscripts. For we can discover two different kinds of text at this time.

(i) In Egypt (from which our earliest manuscripts, being papyrus, come) and probably in Palestine and Syria too, there were lively traditions of preserving texts in a scholarly way. These had been developed in the preservation of the Greek classics, especially Homer: and although we do not know the names of the Christian scholars who did it, it is clear that someone used the same methods of study and editing for the New Testament since this had now become corrupt in places. So some of our texts have evidently been carefully edited. Since the editors understood the type of corruption to which any writing is liable, these texts are, on the whole, good texts; but since even editors can make mistakes and alterations, these are to be found too to some degree.

(ii) On the other hand, texts were preserved in other places such as in western Europe and in Syria dating from the days when corruption and error were rife. Such are the texts quoted in early writers or found in manuscripts which combine both Greek and Latin texts. These contain much incorrect material: but sometimes a true reading will survive there, which has disappeared in the edited texts.

Naturally, the edited texts gained predominance in the Greek-speaking world: the text of Alexandria mainly in Egypt, where it probably persisted until the Arab conquest; the text thought to come from Antioch in the rest of the east through the Middle Ages. This is not to say that all other forms of text were blotted out: in fact different families of text continued to be used in the Greek world until at least the ninth century, and copied after that date, but most people used the two texts that we have just mentioned. The main sphere of influence of the corrupt but earlier texts was in the Latin and Syriac areas.

What is true of Paul's letters is true, with some changes, of the rest of the New Testament. The case of the Gospels is more complex. These circulated separately at first, as is shown by the existence of a number of manuscripts containing a single Gospel. It is clear from the quotations of the early Fathers that the texts of the Gospels which they knew were not exactly identical with any that has yet come to light in the manuscripts.

So long as there were people alive who could remember what Jesus and his disciples had said, men often preferred this oral tradition to the written word, or adjusted the written word to agree with what they had heard orally. This is a chief cause of early alteration. There were also other factors at work: for instance, some people thought it more reverent to tone down any strong words or phrases of Jesus, especially if they implied human emotions, or any actions springing from emotion. We have seen an example of this above (p. 123): we might also mention for instance John 6: 15 where most manuscripts read that Jesus 'withdrew': but the original is clearly to be found in those few which say that he 'flees' or 'runs away'. In this period too it is clear that people already had established preferences for one Gospel rather than another, and Matthew was early a clear favourite. Hence the wording of Mark and Luke in parallel passages tended to be altered to agree with that of Matthew. For instance, in the account of the mocking of Jesus, Matthew has in 26: 68 the words 'Now, Messiah, if you are a prophet, tell us who hit you': both Mark 14: 65 and Luke 22: 64 have shorter sentences, which in some manuscripts have been expanded to give the same words as Matthew. This sort of thing happened in some cases as early as the time of Marcion. When the Gospels came to be written in one book (a stage known from late second century evidence) this type of corruption was even stronger than before. In the texts current in the later Middle Ages this feature, called 'harmonization', is particularly clear, and shows in our own Authorized Version.

We find in the Gospels more than elsewhere additions of extra material to the text of some manuscripts. This is derived from the type of oral tradition of which we have spoken: and occasionally arises from other causes. There are two outstanding and striking examples of this. One is the story of the woman taken in the act of adultery, found in some manuscripts after John 7: 59: other manuscripts have it in other places, some in John (after 7: 36 or 21: 24), some in Luke (after 21: 38), while a number of trustworthy and important manuscripts do not have it at all. Even in those which do have it, its precise wording varies considerably: and it is plain that it is not the work of the evangelist. In all, the evidence points to the fact that this fine story of Jesus's compassion and insight is one not used by any evangelist, but that it was current orally in the early days of the Church. It was inevitable that certain scribes should at length make up for the oversight of the evangelists and insert it. The other striking example is the 'last twelve verses of Mark' (16: 9–20): these are not found in a number of important manuscripts, while in others an alternative rather shorter ending is found or has been added. Here too the addition is shown by its style not to be the work of the evangelist. In this case it seems that the Gospel by intention or accident ends very abruptly: in early days this lack was made good by composing different endings, one of which became well known and much used.

Other additions are not so lengthy. There is an addition after Matt. 27: 49 describing the stabbing of the side of Jesus (before his death. Contrast John 19: 34). After Luke 6: 4, there is a story of Jesus's words to a man seen digging on the sabbath, 'man, if you know what you are doing, you are blessed: but if you do not, you are cursed and one who breaks the law'. After the first part of Luke 22: 19, there are words drawn from 1 Corinthians 11 to supplement an apparently incomplete account of the Lord's Supper. After John 5: 3, there is an explanation of the term 'the disturbance of the water' by an account of the angel's action in troubling it. There are very few cases, of which that in Luke 6 may be one, where the additions prove on close examination to be part of the original wording. But many of them, because they explained obscurities or added interesting and picturesque detail were kept in the later forms of the text.

The Acts of the Apostles also presents a difficult problem to the student of the text because here we find two early very different editions. One is contained in the western manuscripts, both Greek and Latin. The other is known in manuscripts of the type of text originating in Alexandria. The later texts present us with a compromise between the two. The so-called Western text is much longer and has many additions. Sometimes interesting detail was added; for instance, at 11: 28 the sentence is recast to include the words 'when we were gathered together', showing that the author was a Syrian of Antioch. Sometimes material was supplied which later generations thought necessary to complete a story; for instance 8: 37 is a phrase which was added to bring the account into conformity with the conduct of baptisms in a later age, and at 21: 2 after the word 'Patara' the words 'and Myra' were added, which appear to make the account of the stages of such a journey more accurate and probable. Sometimes references to the Holy Spirit were introduced; for instance at 15: 29 where in addition to other differences the 'Western' text reads 'if you keep yourselves free from these things you will be doing right, led by the Holy Spirit'.

This longer text has had its supporters amongst scholars, and there can be no doubt that in Acts as elsewhere this text is sometimes right. But neither text is pure and much more study is needed before we fully understand the way in which the text of Acts developed. For instance, there are such unsolved problems as the following. The Chester Beatty papyrus of Acts has a text not identical with that of either of these main groups: but it is too fragmentary to allow us to draw any far-reaching conclusions from it. Nor do the earliest Fathers help very much since Acts is not a book which lends itself to much quotation, or to use for proving a theological point. Perhaps this is one reason why it could be changed so radically at an early date.

In the Letters of James, Peter, John and Jude there does not seem to have been so much change in general, although one interpolation has become notorious and has occasioned fierce and vituperous controversy. This is the insertion of a sentence after 1 John 5: 6 concerning the 'three heavenly witnesses', that is, the Holy Trinity. This is a Latin insertion but it has influenced three late and obscure Greek manuscripts: in this way it came to be printed in the earliest editions, for example, the Authorized Version where it reads: 'For there are three that bear record in heaven, the Father, the Word, and the Holy Ghost: and these three are one'. It seemed to be a part of the original until scholarship revealed the sources from which it was derived.

The Book of Revelation did not come down to us without change: all the factors already spoken of were at work but one is predominant, the tendency to amend its peculiar Greek which is moulded so strongly on a Hebrew or Aramaic model that it has practically its own syntax. Many of the variations which occur are attempts to make this language conform to normal Greek and these variations are not haphazard in their occurrence.

OUR KNOWLEDGE TODAY

As we have seen, the type of text which is a compromise between the older types finally became dominant in about the tenth century, a time of scholarly and literary activity in the court and learned circles at Constantinople. Most of the manuscripts which came into western Europe at the close of the Middle Ages were of this type. The scholars who printed texts of the Greek Testament—such men as Erasmus at Basel, Cardinal Ximenes at Alcala, Robert Estienne in Paris—had to rely upon the manuscripts which happened to be available to them. They were men of scholarship, but they had no way of choosing between variant readings even when they were aware of them. Thus the earliest printed texts give us a late medieval text of the New Testament, and the great Reformation translations are based on these. The text is not so corrupt that it obscures the essential gospel: but it could not become the basis of precise historical study and comment. Nor were the men of that day aware as we are of the type of Greek in which the New Testament is written. For these two reasons, it has been evident for almost a century that the Authorized Version of 1611 can no longer be fully acceptable as an accurate translation of the Greek, simply because it is not translated from a sound Greek text.

During the seventeenth century men became aware of the mass of variation between manuscripts and translations and Fathers. Much material was published, for instance by Bishop Brian Walton in his great Polyglot Bible of 1653–7 (polyglot = in many languages) and by John Mills in his Greek New Testament, published in 1707, which was the first to list all the variations then known. Throughout the eighteenth century men collected more variants, and increased their knowledge of manuscripts and versions: in the nineteenth century, the search was extended further east, and from Sinai and Jerusalem scholars like Constantine Tischendorf brought back material older than any known till then. Meanwhile the analysis and theorizing went on, improving as it took account of newly discovered facts, until the Cambridge scholars Westcott and Hort in 1881 produced the text which they boldly called the New Testament in the original Greek. Most scholars today would agree that this was too much to claim: but nevertheless Westcott and Hort had produced a scholarly edition which represents in the main the kind of text used in Alexandria, in the late third or early fourth century. This was a great improvement on earlier editions, and very valuable to students of the Bible.

All these things led to the revision of the standard English translation, the Authorized Version (see p. 5). The Revised Version, as it was called, was an attempt to combine the revered and familiar beauty of the Authorized Version with the new advances in textual criticism and knowledge of New Testament Greek. The present century has seen a number of private attempts at new translation which have mainly followed the text of Westcott and Hort. But today, as this chapter will have shown, there has taken place a shift of opinion from the acceptance of a text of any one manuscript, recension or scholar, to a realization that the earliest days of the text are still to some extent unknown to us. This leaves scholars more free to choose between variations on grounds of rational argument, and to try to clear up points of difficulty. This is why the translators of the New English Bible have taken it upon themselves to establish their own Greek text at a number of crucial points. It must never be forgotten that it is a debatable matter whether they have succeeded in arriving at the original in all instances.

Similarly, our knowledge of the Greek of the New Testament has made great progress since 1881 (the date of Westcott and Hort), due mainly to two advances; first in the knowledge of everyday Greek which the papyri have made possible; secondly, in the detailed study of the Greek of the Septuagint Old Testament, which was the Bible of the early Christian Greek-speaking church and has influenced New Testament usage and vocabulary at many vital points.

So the New Testament has come to us from the days of its composition and compilation: it has been often copied and commented upon, from time to time corrupted, as a rule by well-meaning folk, but there have always been means of scholarship to check and remove corruption and to approach nearer to the original words of the apostles and the men of their age. Men of consecrated learning—in Alexandria and Caesarea, in

Constantinople, at the Renaissance, in western Europe and indeed throughout the world in our days—have pursued the quest of that text. Today, standing on the shoulders of giants of the past we are able to see the history of the text more clearly than they; we understand the language with greater precision; we have a text very near to the original.

In no age has the text been so far from its original state that men could not gain from it the witness of the men of Jesus's day to the power and peace which they found in him. But the greater the precision of our knowledge, the more secure will be our certainty and the more wonderful the sight of him which we derive from the New Testament's words.

5

WHAT THE NEW TESTAMENT IS ABOUT

THE NEW TESTAMENT AND THE OLD TESTAMENT

The New English Bible is to be a new translation of both the Old and the New Testaments and it will use, as all Bibles have done for many centuries, these two sub-titles. As we have seen already, the specifically Christian books which are in the New Testament were gathered together under that title because of the conviction that a new covenant, or testament, has been made; this is the main theme of the books. Because of this the scriptures of the Jewish church have become, for Christians, the Old Testament. Christ, says one writer, 'is the mediator of a new covenant, or testament, under which, now that there has been a death to bring deliverance from sins committed under the former covenant, those whom God has called may receive the promise of the eternal inheritance' (Heb. 9: 15). This same writer has already referred back to the prophet's declaration that 'The days are coming, says the Lord, when I will conclude a new covenant with the house of Israel and the house of Judah' (Heb. 8: 8; Jer. 31: 31). Then he says, 'By speaking of a new covenant, he has pronounced the first one old; and anything that is growing old and ageing will shortly disappear' (Heb. 8: 13). Why, then, do we keep the Old Testament in the Bible? Surely by now it should have disappeared? If the new covenant really is established, as the New Testament writers all quite firmly believe, why do we go on thinking at all about the old one and preserving in

the Bible the books which were written before the time
of Jesus?

Although we are talking about a new covenant we are
not talking about a new God. Sometimes people think
that God seems so different in the New and the Old
Testaments that they really are about two different gods.
But this is a mistake and not a new one. Marcion made
it in the second century and said that Christians ought to
stop using the old Jewish scriptures. But when, in whatever language or translation, we read in the New Testament about 'the great things God has done' (Acts 2: 11)
these are the new things that the same God has done.

The Jews had learned to believe that there is only one
God; they believed that he had been active throughout
their history, showing himself to be both powerful and
good. They differed from many of their neighbours in
believing these things. Not only had they learned to
believe that 'the Lord our God is one Lord' (Deut. 6: 4),
they had also come to understand that he is profoundly
concerned about all human affairs. This is not taken for
granted by any means in all religions; there are many
people for whom the idea of a god or gods means some
distant power who is 'against' rather than 'for' human
beings or more likely just neutral and not caring either
way. Scattered about in other countries as they were in
the centuries before Jesus's day, the Jews could not help
discovering how different their religion was from those
of other nations. Naturally they reflected on these
things. How was it that they were different? They
believed themselves to be specially bound in loyalty to
God and that he was specially concerned for them in all
their life and history. This faith for the present and for the
future was rooted in their interpretation of the past. They

believed that their forefathers, led by Moses, God's servant, had been rescued from slavery in a foreign land and they believed that this was a mark of God's favour towards them and also an indication that he had a special purpose for them.

Some of them believed that all this was just a mark of special favour, giving them special privileges. Others came to believe that it was their destiny to be the people who should declare to the world the true nature of God, his love and his mercy, and his demands upon all mankind for loyalty and obedience. 'I the Lord have called thee in righteousness, and will hold thine hand, and will keep thee, and give thee for a covenant of the people, for a light of the Gentiles; to open the blind eyes, to bring out the prisoners from the dungeon, and them that sit in darkness out of the prison house' (Isa. 42: 6, 7).

All this is implied by using the word covenant to describe the relationship between God and his people. The word was originally used for solemn agreements between man and man, but when it was used to express the bond between God and man it inevitably took on a special sense.

The Jews who believed these things were also acutely aware that Israel had failed to measure up to such a high calling. But they still believed that although Israel had failed to fulfil her covenant obligations God would stand by his word and would not reject her. So it came about that they expected God to take strong and decisive action, as he had done before when Pharaoh was the oppressor, to establish Israel as an independent nation. Then she would be free to carry out her mission to the rest of the world, to declare to all peoples the one God, his love, his righteousness and his power.

While they waited for this to happen they had their part to play, particularly by studying the scriptures and interpreting the old commandments for their own times to try to ensure that people obeyed them. This Jewish faith was firmly held and devoutly practised by Jews living in most countries around the eastern Mediterranean, including Palestine itself. Jesus was born into this society and brought up in this religion. The only story which has come down to us about his boyhood, apart from apocryphal ones, is about the time when his parents took him to Jerusalem for the Passover festival when he was twelve years old (Luke 2: 41–9). When the festival season was over the rest of the party set off for home and then they discovered that Jesus was missing. They went back to look for him and when they found him 'in the temple surrounded by the teachers' he asked them, 'What made you search?...Did you not know that I was bound to be in my Father's house?' If we had no Old Testament should we not be wondering what these teachers were teaching and who Jesus meant by 'my Father'? This is just one example of the way in which the great Jewish teaching about God is taken for granted throughout the New Testament. We have already seen how the Christians used the old scriptures and how important it was to them to establish that prophecy had been fulfilled.

When the writer to the Hebrews talks about the old disappearing he is talking about the old way the Jews had thought about their own relationship to God, the terms of the agreement which they believed had been made in the past, particularly through Moses and the Law. The New Testament is about a new understanding and a new agreement, based on new understanding of the nature of God because of the new thing he has done and the new life he has brought by revealing himself in Jesus Christ. So the Old Testament scriptures remain scripture for Christians because of their witness to God as creator and ruler in history and because they prepare the way for new history. But the old covenant of which they tell is superseded by a new covenant, as indeed some prophets expected it would be. The New Testament tells about the way this new agreement was made, what it cost and what its terms are.

THE MESSAGE OF SALVATION

The salvation for which most of the Jews had been hoping was salvation from the Romans. They were waiting for the Messiah who would win this freedom for them. 'We had been hoping that he was the man to liberate Israel' (Luke 24: 21), they said of Jesus; and again, while they were talking with him for the last time, 'Lord, is this the time when you are to establish once again the sovereignty of Israel?' (Acts 1: 6). But this was not his role, he made no moves in this direction and the claim that Jesus was the Messiah must have seemed just ludicrous to people who were expecting the Messiah to save Israel by restoring her political freedom. If this is the work of the Messiah then Jesus was not the Messiah; if Jesus is the Messiah, crucified and raised from death and now exalted, then Messiah means something different from what most people had meant by it.

There is some difficulty about the use of this word Messiah in the Gospels: sometimes it is used, sometimes it seems to be avoided: even if there was not a problem about its meaning during Jesus's ministry there certainly was one by the time the Gospels were written. But in spite of the ambiguity the Christians went on using the word: it was because they used it so much, in its Greek form 'Christ', that they 'got the name of Christians' (Acts 11: 26). They used this title for Jesus because it was the right and proper title for God's anointed, the one who brings salvation. But the preaching that got them their nickname was the proclamation of deliverance from the power of sin. The Jews had hoped to be saved from the Romans, but sin hinders God's purposes far more than the Romans did!

We have seen that the Jews were nevertheless conscious of their failure, their sin, their weakness as an instrument for the purposes of God, their need of deliverance and salvation if they were to be able to become his more faithful people. They had hoped that in the end some sort of reconciliation might be made, that God would be prepared to accept them on the basis of their repentance and amendment and then he would bring in the new covenant. Christians say 'upon us the fulfilment of the ages has come' (1 Cor. 10: 11) and refer back to 'the message of the truth, the good news of your salvation' (Eph. 1: 13). The good news of the gospel is that the new covenant is made. God has given new hope to man through Jesus Christ, his life, his death, and his triumphant resurrection. This is the message of all the books of the New Testament and—more astonishing still—this message is not for Jews only.

The Jews who had believed that Israel was called to be God's ambassador to the world had expected that the other nations would come to realize that the truth was with them and would ask to be associated with them and so come to live in obedience to God's will. 'Ten men... out of all the languages of the nations, shall even take hold of the skirt of him that is a Jew, saying, We will go with you, for we have heard that God is with you' (Zech. 8: 23). All mankind is sinful, even if all do not describe the sense of failure and conflict in terms of disobedience to the revealed will of God. The Christian message is that through Jesus Christ God offers salvation to all men. Most of the Jews denied that Jesus was the Messiah in any sense: they did not believe that there is any message of salvation for anybody. And not all of those who did accept Jesus as Messiah and came to be called Christians thought that it was right that the message should be proclaimed to gentiles as well as Jews. This preaching to gentiles did not happen at the very beginning but by the time the New Testament books came to be written it had begun, and grave controversy had broken out within the Church: in Paul's earliest letters there are clear signs of this. But the evangelist Matthew had inherited a tradition that Jesus had said, 'Go forth therefore and make all nations my disciples' (Matt. 28: 19). The Gospels are mainly concerned with the figure of Jesus as he had lived out his mission and with the events leading up to his death. The other books in the New Testament are mostly about the meaning of what has happened and the working out of the implications of the new beliefs, both in theory and in practice. In their various ways all the writers have the same object, clearly expressed by the one who says that he has written 'in order that you may hold the faith that Jesus is the Christ, the Son of God, and that through this faith you may possess eternal life by his name' (John 20: 31).

OUR LORD JESUS CHRIST

What kind of evidence do these writers offer to encourage us to think that they were right? One thing they do is to tell us about some of the things which Jesus said and did in his lifetime which struck people and made them think there was something unusual about him. He had a characteristic way of teaching. In those days people had come to depend almost entirely on professional scribes for the interpretation of their scriptures and for religious and moral guidance. Against this very rigid background Jesus taught the people and went on to say things like: 'But what do you think about this?' (Matt. 21: 28), 'Which of these three do you think was neighbour to the man who fell into the hands of the robbers?' (Luke 10: 36). These questions were put seriously and they need answers. Often the answers seem to us obvious enough, the questions scarcely worth asking because there can only be one answer. But actually to give the answer demands more than just seeing what it is: giving the answer involves acting on it. 'Go and do as he did' (Luke 10: 37), said Jesus to the lawyer; it was his way of telling the lawyer that he had given a good answer. Jesus was not inviting clever original answers, although sometimes the obvious answer implies something which challenges generally accepted standards. The important thing about the asking of the question is that it invites everyone who hears it not only to answer it but to act on it. Jesus's way of teaching encouraged people to think for themselves about the right things to do instead of just obeying rules blindly. By doing this he fulfilled the prophet's idea of God's promise: 'I will put my law in their inward parts, and in their heart will I write it; and

I will be their God, and they shall be my people'
(Jer. 31: 33).

Jesus set people thinking not only by the things he said
but by the things he did. In some ways it seemed that his
whole ministry was in warm harmony with the beliefs
and hopes of the Jews. In other ways his teaching and his
behaviour clashed violently with what was commonly
accepted. He was prepared to have dealings with all sorts
of people, including those to whom respectable people
would not speak. He was aware that people criticized him
for being 'a friend of tax-gatherers and sinners' (Matt.
11: 19; Luke 7: 34); and he did not keep all the rules
which the scribes laid down so that 'the president of the
synagogue' was 'indignant with Jesus for healing on the
Sabbath' (Luke 13: 14).

When Jesus asked his disciples 'Who do you say I
am?' (Matt. 16: 15; Mark 8: 29; Luke 9: 20) he presumably did it because he knew that people were discuss-
ing him because of what he said and did and he wanted
the disciples to tell him what they were thinking. In
these three Gospels the story is told of the question being
asked and of Peter saying Jesus was the Messiah. The other
features of the three stories are different. In John's
Gospel we read that on another occasion 'some of the
people said, "This must certainly be the expected
prophet." Others said, "This is the Messiah"' (John 7: 40,
41). We are also told that he spoke and acted with an
authority which was unmistakable but yet not like anything they had known before. They asked him, 'By
what authority are you acting like this? Who gave you
authority to act in this way?' (Mark 11: 28). If we can
think ourselves back into the time of Jesus's ministry,
before his death and resurrection, we can begin to under-

stand what a real and urgent question this must have been. It is just as real and urgent a question for us too. 'Who do you say I am?' is a much more searching question than just 'Are you with me or against me?', or 'Which side are you on?'

Most people who trouble to study the New Testament at all do so because they believe at least that it contains valuable teaching and that Jesus was a notable and heroic figure. But it is difficult to read the book itself without coming up against the fundamental question. Originally the stark question was 'Is he or is he not the Messiah? has he or has he not authority from God?' The New Testament books were written by people who believed that the answers were definitely 'Yes, and yes, and more besides'. They wrote what they wrote so that others might share their belief and understand the reasons for their faith. Ever since then the question has been 'Was their faith justified? Were their reasons sound?' So we have the strange paradox that although the question has been answered, and answered with deep conviction, still it remains to be answered, for we have to answer it for ourselves. And it remains with us because the answers that have been given involve the use of words which themselves raise further questions: the phrase 'Son of God', for instance, implies a reaching out beyond the range of what man can fully comprehend: the phrase 'Son of Man' carries with it profound questions about the nature of man. These underlying questions about God and man have always been live questions and they still are in the present day. If the answer which the New Testament gives to the fundamental question about Jesus is the true one it has infinitely far-reaching implications. Generation after generation of Christians have handed down both their own conviction and the gospel tradition which puts the question to their successors, 'Who do *you* say I am?' Studying the New Testament means living with this question, growing in understanding of its meaning and of the meaning of some of the answers that have been given.

The question which follows on after this one is 'What did he do?' and another question which must have been particularly urgent for the first Christians is 'Why did he have to die like that?' By the time the New Testament books were written an answer given to the second question seems to have provided part of the answer to the first. Plenty of people would have been found saying that Jesus had deserved the shameful death of crucifixion, that the charges of blasphemy and treason which had been brought against him were proved and that he had quite properly been put to death because of his misdeeds. But Christians came to say 'He was delivered to death for *our* misdeeds' and they evidently did not just mean that it was their fault that he had been caught, because they go on to say 'and raised to life to justify us' (Rom. 4: 25).

This gives part of an answer to 'What did he do?', but what did Paul mean by saying that Jesus had been raised to life 'to justify us'? He is talking about the same thing in his speech at Pisidian Antioch when he says: 'you must understand, my brothers, that it is through him that forgiveness of sins is now being proclaimed to you. It is through him that everyone who has faith is acquitted of everything for which there was no acquittal under the Law of Moses' (Acts 13: 38, 39). The old covenant had been broken, there was no acquittal; now there is acquittal, the new covenant is made. They did not all believe it: obviously people who did not believe that

Jesus was Messiah, or that God had raised him from death, did not believe either in the forgiveness of sins which was being proclaimed. But believers 'are not among those who shrink back and are lost; we have the faith to make life our own' (Heb. 10: 39).

THE NEW BEGINNING

People who believe that the new covenant has been made and that forgiveness is really offered believe that they have been enlisted by God for the job of making this good news known. Their faith is rooted in history. Christianity is not a historical religion just in the sense that it comes from the past, or that it is associated with a historical character, or even that it emphasizes the importance of history. It is historical in the sense that it stems from the belief that within history itself, in a particular place, at a particular time, God himself took a hand in a totally unprecedented fashion. Although this is something which happened in the past it is not just past history; at any rate not for Christians, because they believe that the Spirit of the risen Jesus is still here carrying on with the work of deliverance and salvation.

This is a tremendous thing to believe and many people do not think it possible that the Christian interpretation of the life and work of Jesus can be true. But there have been very many who have believed that it is true and have set out to discover what it means for every aspect of human living. These men of faith have included a great and notable variety of human beings, all claiming to be 'built upon the foundation laid by the apostles and prophets, and Christ Jesus himself is the foundation-stone' (Eph. 2: 20). Working out the implications of Christian belief is a difficult task, so it is not surprising that Christians have disagreed with one another, sometimes violently.

It stands to reason that anything so startling as saying that God raised Jesus to life again after death challenges people who are presented with it to look afresh at all the things they have believed about God before. Practically always when the word 'God' is used in the New Testament it means God as the Jews then believed in him, one almighty God, creator of the world and ruler of history, who had called their forefathers to be a special people. They believed that they were the inheritors of this calling and that God who had delivered his people once would deliver them again. The Christian proclamation was that he had acted and revealed himself in a new way, that he had delivered them from the burden of their past and given them a profounder understanding of the range of his power and the depth of his love. So Christians inherit much of what Jews had already believed, but they inherit it in a state of being transformed.

When ideas about God are changing radically because something so new has broken in, ideas about man and about man's relation to God may have to be changed too and with them the whole pattern of religion. There will be new ways of speaking about God, about mankind, about the present and the future and perhaps most of all about religion. All the new ideas could not be worked out immediately, certainly not during the time before the New Testament books were written. Probably this is something which can never be completely done. The coming of Jesus Christ was the beginning of the new history of salvation which is still going on and we are in this history just as we are all in history in the ordinary sense.

This does not mean that God's work is not in one sense completed: we are told that shortly before his death, as he hung upon the cross, Jesus said, 'It is accomplished!' (John 19: 30) and indeed there was a most wonderful completeness about everything that he did, both in life and in death. But after this was over, even after they began to be aware that he was alive again, everyday life for most people most of the time was just as it had always been. Yet the disciples were absolutely certain that something epoch-making had happened and they wondered what they ought to be doing about it. This is one of the things they could not see immediately, beyond the obvious thing of telling other people about it. But as time went on they learned, and this is the sort of thing they said: 'the old order has gone, and a new order has already begun. From first to last this has been the work of God. He has reconciled us men to himself through Christ, and he has enlisted us in this service of reconciliation. What I mean is, that God was in Christ reconciling the world to himself, no longer holding men's misdeeds against them, and that he has entrusted us with the message of reconciliation' (2 Cor. 5: 17b–19). And 'God is love; and his love was disclosed to us in this, that he sent his only Son into the world to bring us life. The love I speak of is not our love for God, but the love he showed to us in sending his Son as the remedy for the defilement of our sins. If God thus loved us, dear friends, we in turn are bound to love one another' (1 John 4: 8–11).

THE HOLY SPIRIT OF GOD

The meaning of God's great work in Jesus Christ has been gradually unfolding ever since it was first proclaimed, history has been moving on all the time, man's horizons have extended enormously and his problems have become more and more complex. While all this has been going on many ideas and beliefs have been discarded and many others have had to be reshaped: this process is still going on. Of course many people think that the Christian beliefs themselves are out of date and ought to be discarded: and if they are out of date they certainly ought to be discarded. But the more clearly people see what these beliefs actually are the more they see how important they must be for every period of history and for all kinds of people—if they are true. This, after all, is the only criterion; the trouble is that the test of truth is difficult to apply here. A lot of work can be done to test the historical facts which are involved, but what matters is whether the explanations of the facts are true or not and this is something which cannot be tested in the same way at all. The matter just cannot be settled one way or the other like that. If the message of salvation is the truth it ought to be a most welcome message, because there can be no doubt about man's need to be delivered from all the many things which hinder his good living, strife, fear, hate, envy, greed, indeed from all his sins.

When people believe that forgiveness and reconciliation are really offered they live their lives in faith—they believe that God is as the New Testament writers say he is and that he has done what they say he has done. This is not just wishful thinking—they do not believe just because this is a comforting faith to have—they live like this because they believe that the gospel is the truth. This life of faith is a strenuous affair; this too is clear from the New Testament. Continually every part of life has to be looked at from this point of view, decisions have to be taken and put into effect on this basis.

Christians have been going on like this for a long time: the Christian Church has many centuries of history behind her and it is easy to point to her failures, both corporate and individual, as people often do. But failure is not the whole story: she has grown and she has been a powerful influence, often for very great good, recognized as good even by those who do not accept her beliefs. At the very beginning the Christians did not expect history to go on like this; they thought a dramatic end would come quite soon and a quite new world would begin. But instead of enjoying salvation in a totally different environment they found themselves learning to live it out in the old familiar world. Learning to live it out in our world means an enormous amount of work, learning, teaching, preaching, building up good relationships, good organization, good government—everything which serves the needs of man. It means studying many other questions. How do we bring the message of salvation? Why does everything take so long? Has everybody got to be Christian before things get better? Do things necessarily get better if people are Christians? Although God has taken away from man his bondage to sin he has not taken away his freedom to choose and so we still make all kinds of mistakes and hinder God's purposes. But God, it seems, has faith in man, that he can learn to co-operate and play his part in bringing life and health and peace.

'We speak of these gifts of God in words found for us not by our human wisdom but by the Spirit' (1 Cor.

2: 13). This is typical of the way the New Testament writers speak about the Spirit. They talk of Jesus being 'led away by the Spirit' (Matt. 4: 1), 'armed with the power of the Spirit' (Luke 4: 14) and later on they say of Christians that they 'became incorporate in Christ and received the seal of the promised Holy Spirit' (Eph. 1: 13). And Paul said to the Galatian Christians 'the harvest of the Spirit is love, joy, peace, patience, kindness, goodness, fidelity, gentleness, and self-control' (Gal. 5: 22, 23). And 'If the Spirit is the source of our life, let the Spirit also direct our course' (Gal. 5: 25). This was not a new idea in itself, the Spirit of God is frequently spoken about in the Old Testament as inspiring prophets and others: 'the spirit of the Lord shall rest upon him, the spirit of wisdom and understanding, the spirit of counsel and might, the spirit of knowledge and of the fear of the Lord' (Isa. 11: 2) and some looked forward to the time when these gifts would be more widespread. Christians claim that this time has come. Peter says that 'this is what the prophet spoke of: "God says, 'This will happen in the last days: I will pour out upon everyone a portion of my spirit; and your sons and daughters shall prophesy; your young men shall see visions, and your old men shall dream dreams'"' (Acts 2: 16, 17; Joel 2: 28, 29). So the earliest Christians were confident that they were incorporated in Christ and strengthened and inspired by the Holy Spirit of God for their work of proclaiming the message of salvation. It has been the same ever since; those who live by faith are always at full stretch, all their skills and abilities are called into play and at the same time they believe that God works in and through what they do, all the time teaching them to understand more clearly what is his will and how we can be taken up into the working out of his purposes. 'It is God who works in you, inspiring both the will and the deed, for his own chosen purpose' (Phil. 2: 13).

The objectives and ideals of human life are not noticeably different under the new covenant from what they were before. But there is new hope of achieving them and some very different ideas about methods of working for them. God's method of bringing in the new order was so totally unexpected that people could scarcely recognize at the time what had happened. Many still do not believe it. But the New Testament tells us how God brought justification out of condemnation, life out of death, faith and hope out of despair. The first believers began to understand and to learn to live in the new way. They recognized that God's Holy Spirit was teaching them and giving them courage and enthusiasm, creating a body of people to do the work of the gospel. They responded to the call to move out beyond Judaea and Samaria and Galilee where Jesus had worked and where they had first preached and so the mission to the world opened up. 'So these two, sent out on their mission by the Holy Spirit, came down to Seleucia, and from there sailed to Cyprus. Arriving at Salamis, they declared the word of God in the Jewish synagogues' (Acts 13: 4, 5). As they spread out and new questions came up, like the one about preaching to people who were not Jews, they tackled them in the same spirit of confidence and courage. 'It is the decision of the Holy Spirit, and our decision, to lay no further burden upon you beyond these essentials' (Acts 15: 28). Some of the letters which Paul and others wrote, many of which were written because of the problems and disagreements, were kept. Later on the substance of the preaching was written down too, with the traditions about what Jesus had said and done during his ministry which had gathered round it.

Since then the work has gone on, the work of preachers and teachers and scholars right down to the present day. Some Christians have understood their contribution to the work to be in preserving, translating and expounding the New Testament and some are occupied in helping others to read and understand it better. 'When Philip ran up he heard him reading the prophet Isaiah and said, "Do you understand what you are reading?" He said, "How can I understand unless someone will give me the clue?" So he asked Philip to get in and sit beside him' (Acts 8: 30, 31).

INDEX

Actium, battle of, 44
Acts of the Apostles, 93, 117, 130, 139, 140
of Andrew, 111
of John, 111
of Paul, 111
of Paul and Thecla, 111
of Peter, 111
of Thomas, 111
Aelia Capitolina, 63
African Latin version, 132
Agrippa I, 59, 60
Alcimus, 30, 31, 32, 34, 35
Alexander the Great, 16, 18, 21, 124
Alexander Jannaeus, 37, 39, 47
Alexander, son of Aristobulus II, 41
Alexander, son of Herod the Great and Mariamne, 50
Alexandra, queen, 39
Alexandria, founded by Alexander the Great, 18
  Jewish community there, 20, 24, 35, 60
  Christian scholars at work, 133, 136, 139, 142, 143
allegory, 82, 108
American Standard Version, 5
Antigonus, son of Aristobulus II, 41, 42
Antioch, Pisidian, 46, 97
Antioch, Syrian, 21, 69, 79, 136
Antiochus I, 21
Antiochus III, the Great, 21, 26
Antiochus IV, Epiphanes, 22, 26–32
Antiochus V, 30, 34
Antipater, governor of Idumaea, 39–42
Antipater, son of Herod the Great and Doris, 50
Antonia, fort, 48
Antony, 42, 44
apocalypse, 102, 103, 111
apocrypha, 109–11, 148
apologetic, 101

apostles' proclamation, see proclamation
apostolic Fathers, see Fathers
Arab conquest, 136
Arabic version, 132
Aramaic language, 22, 66, 74, 124
Archelaus, son of Herod the Great and Malthace, 50–4
Aretas, king, 40
Aristeas, letter of, 22, 36
Aristobulus I, 37
Aristobulus II, son of Alexander Jannaeus, 39–41, 44
Aristobulus, son of Herod the Great and Mariamne, 50
Aristotle, 16
Armenian version, 132
Asia, 16, 26, 48, 102, 132
Athanasius, bishop of Alexandria, 104, 105, 120
Athens, 16
Augustus, emperor, 44–7, 50–4
Authorized Version, 3, 138, 140, 142

Babylon and the Babylonians, 11–13, 16, 21
baptism, 57, 67, 70, 95, 96
Bar-Cochba, 63
Barnabas, letter of, 106–8, 117, 120
Baruch, book of, 103
Berenice, 50
Bodmer papyri, 127
Britain, 44

Caesarea, 47, 61, 79, 133, 143
Caesarean text, 133
Caligula, 59, and see Gaius
canon, 105
Carrhae, battle of, 41
Casey, Robert, 125
Chasidim, see Hasidaeans
Chenoboskion, 110
Chester Beatty papyri, 127, 140
Christians, a distinctive group, 63, 66, 67, 96, 97

INDEX

their name, 69, 150

Church, growing, 6, 7, 65, 79
God's People, 113
writings, 119, 120

churches, 65

circumcision, 14, 80

Claudius, emperor, 55, 60, 62

Clement of Alexandria, 74

Clement, bishop of Rome, 106, 114, 135

I Clement, 106, 114, 117, 120

II Clement, 106

codex, 127

Codex Sinaiticus, 128

Colossae, 114

Constantinople, 126, 141, 144

Coptic versions, 110, 130, 134

Corinth, 86, 106, 114

corruption of the text, 122, 134, 136, 138, 143

covenant, 7, 8, 99, 147
the old, 64, 149, 155
the new, 8, 63, 64, 101, 150, 155, 156

covenanters, 33, 56

Crassus, 41

critical apparatus, 134

cursive manuscripts, 126

Cyprian, bishop of Carthage, 133

Damascus, land of, 32, 33

Damasus, Pope, 130

Daniel, book of, 30, 32, 102

Danube, river, 44

David, king, 25, 37, 56

Dead Sea scrolls, 32, 99

Decapolis, 54

Dedication, festival of, 29

Demetrius, son of Seleucus IV, 34, 36

Diatessaron, 115, 130

didache, 88, 89, 101

Didache, or Teaching of the Twelve
Apostles, 94, 106, 107

Diognētus, letter to, 106, 108, 117

dispersion, 11, 20, 36, 46, 55

Doris, wife of Herod the Great, 50

Egypt, Jews living there, 13, 31, 36
ruled by Ptolemies, 18
manuscripts, 126, 127, 136

Elasa, battle of, 34

Eleazar, 62

Enoch, book of, 103

Ephesus, 84

Erasmus, 141

Essenes, 33

Estienne, Robert, 141

Ethiopic version, 132

ethnarch, 42, 54

euangelion, 72

Eucharist, *see* Lord's Supper

Euphrates, river, 44

Europe, 2, 136, 141, 144

Eusebius, bishop of Caesarea, 73, 76, 113, 116

evangelist, 72

Ezra, 12, 13, 24, 25

Fathers, 105, 132, 137, 142

Felix, governor, 61

Festus, governor, 61

Gaius, emperor, 59, 60

Galatia, 86

Galilee, 38, 54, 57, 58, 81

Gaul, 129

gentiles, 37, 84, 151

Georgian version, 132, 133

Gerizim, Mount, 21, 38

gnōsis, gnostic, 84, 110

gospel, 88, 118, 141

Gospel of Matthew, 72, 78, 79, 114–117, 137
of Mark, 72, 78, 114–117, 137
of Luke, 72, 114–117, 137
of John, 65, 114–117
of Thomas, 110
of Thomas (Syriac), 109, 111
of Peter, 109, 116

Gothic version, 132

Greece and the Greeks, 11, 16, 18

Greek language, 2, 16, 18, 22, 23, 124, 143

165

INDEX